LIMITLESS INTIMACY

LIMITLESS INTIMACY

A Guide to Spiritual Sex

Narecia Hamrick, Ph.D.
&
Grant Bingeman, P.E.

Elysian Press

This book reflects the authors' spiritual or religious beliefs and experiences and is not intended to be therapeutic. Some individuals with different beliefs may find the book objectionable and may wish to avoid reading it. The vignettes are verbatim transcriptions, but identifying material has been removed in order to preserve confidentiality.

LIMITLESS INTIMACY
A GUIDE TO SPIRITUAL SEX

Narecia Hamrick & Grant Bingeman

Copyright (c) 1988, 1989, 1990

All Rights Reserved. No portion of this book may be reproduced without written permission from the authors.

Library of Congress Catalog Card Number 90-81101
ISBN 0-9626562-0-8

For orders and inquiries contact:
Elysian Press
P. O. Box 180158
Dallas, Texas 75218

Illustrated by George R. Holman, Dallas, Texas

Edited by Inez G. Earle, Dallas, Texas

For Our Children

*and for everyone who has yearned
to share more intimacy and ecstacy*

ACKNOWLEDGEMENTS

Individuals who have contributed to this book are too numerous to mention. In one sense, everyone who has ever touched our lives has helped create *Limitless Intimacy*. We are grateful for all relationships which helped inspire our creativity. A special thanks goes to those individuals who have shared their personal experiences with us and are the source of the vignettes throughout the book. Many excellent transcripts had to be omitted for lack of space, but we are grateful for those also, because they helped mold the book in numerous ways.

Thanks are due those persons who contributed to the manuscript style, printing and editorial work, especially to our editor Inez Earle. We would also like to thank George Holman for the illustrations and for his patience and understanding of the material.

But most of all, we want to thank Ruth Bingeman, beloved friend and wife, for her remarkable patience, understanding, support and encouragement.

Material reprinted with permission of Charles Scribner's Sons, an imprint of Macmillan Publishing Company from *The Spirit of St. Louis* by Charles A. Lindbergh. Copyright 1953 Charles Scribner's Sons; copyright renewed (c) 1981 Anne Morrow Lindbergh.

CONTENTS

Preface   *xiii*

Introduction   *xxi*

1. SAWNKI (Sex As We Now Know It)   1

The Search * Intimacy and Freedom * Pleasure and Orgasm * A Joyful Reminiscence * A Glorious Evolution * An Adolescent Delight * Limitations and Inhibitions * Journey Back to Childhood * Personal Reflections * Affirmations * Selected Readings

2 *Flying High Naturally*   27

The First Step * Awareness and ASCs * Understanding OBEs * Childhood OBEs * Magic and Repressed OBEs * Anesthesia and Near-death OBEs * OBEs Motivated by Necessity * Multifaceted OBEs * Environmentally Induced OBEs * Characteristics of OBEs * A Fun Recall of Childhood OBEs * Affirmations * Selected Readings

3. *Relaxing Into Peaceful Expectations*   55

A Tantalizing Invitation * An OBE Invited by Relaxing * Stress and Tension * The Relaxation Response * A Love Exercise * A Personal Relaxation Ritual * A Relaxed Lifestyle * A Commune with Nature * A Simple Miracle * Reconnecting with the Child

* OBE and Flying * Relaxing With Permission * Affirmations * Selected Readings

4. Reawakening Dreams of Rapture — 79

The Potential * A Sexual Rendezvous * Unconscious Mind, Our Teacher * Sharing and Learning * Fascinating Characteristics * Enhancing Dream Recall * Awakening and Entering a Dream * Dream Lovers * Flying Free * The Joy of Dream Sex * Affirmations * Selected Readings

5. Visualizing Pathways to OBS — 101

The Pathways * Our Life Force * Out-of-Body Sex * Shifting Perceptions * A Perceptual Shift Into OBE * Seeing Through Closed Eyes * Abundant Opportunities * Sharing Paths to Ecstasy * Flying Free * Preferred Sensory Modalities * Reactivating Childhood Skills * Return to the Garden of Eden * Mental Sex * Affirmations * Selected Readings

6. Anticipating the Seduction — 123

The Joy of Anticipation * An Invitation to Beauty and Pleasure * Reflections of Our Beauty * An Effortless Seduction * A Tantalizing Love Exercise * Non-Verbal Links to OBS * Creating A Love Ritual * An Energy Triangle * Free and Easy Choices * Affirmations * Selected Readings

7. The Ecstasy of Spiritual Bonding — 141

Our Spiritual Flight * A Sensuous Caress * Kaleidoscopes to OBS * Spiritual Bonding * An Experience of Rapture * Feeling Life As Children * A Journey Beyond Words * Our Magnetic Life Force * Affirming and Letting Go * Freedom and Goodness * Seeds of Ecstasy * Affirmations * Selected Readings

8. Limitless Intimacy — 161

A Blissful State of Awareness * The First Step * Divine Mental Processes * Sharing the Ecstasy * Learning About Pleasure and Intimacy * A Total Union of Souls * Spiritual Bonding * Steps Along the Way * Living in Heaven * Connecting and Loving * The Unborn Potential * An Empathic Group Experience * Expanding Into Limitless Intimacy * Pathways to Limitless Intimacy * Affirmations * Selected Readings

Appendices — 181

Order Form — 187

Author's Biographies — 190

PREFACE

Notes From Narecia:

When asked to write these notes, I found myself reluctant to do so. Perhaps I was simply tired of writing and felt an eagerness for a sense of completion. While writing this book, I have often been blessed with the joy of which I have written. This was especially true during the more creative processes. But after the creative work was completed, certain tasks of analyzing and editing seemed to make it difficult for me to maintain a joyful spiritual awareness. So I was eager to refocus on living in limitless intimacy instead of writing about it.

In spite of my reluctance, I would sincerely like to tell the curious reader how this book evolved. I have been in a lifelong process of spiritual evolution. As a young child I had a strong faith in God. My parents were permissive and allowed me to formulate my own beliefs. I was in awe of nature and felt especially close to God when I was outdoors. I can remember being five or six years old, sitting outside, looking up through the tree branches at the sky and talking to God. My early childhood faith was untrained, but very natural and positive. As I grew older, I received some gentle, Protestant religious training at a local church. Although this religious training was valuable, it also proved to be somewhat limiting and rather confusing.

In college, my education and training in psychology was very scientific and behaviorally oriented. We dealt in observable, measurable events and emphasized the scientific method. During this period, I was drawn to agnosticism because it was consistent with my scientific training and beliefs. So I gave up religion in the name of science. While I was giving up religion, life was busy teaching me about spirituality in very dramatic and meaningful ways. I was exposed to a broad range of emotions and observed very real dramas in romantic and sexual relationships. I was confronted with the mystery and power of the unconscious mind. I had a powerful out-of-body experience, which I discounted and tried to explain in a pseudo-scientific fashion. I met a hypnotist and became fascinated with hypnosis, but remained very skeptical. These and other such events had a lasting effect on my life. Without realizing it, I was being shown pathways and beginning to open doors which would lead me into a new spiritual world — a world in which I had played as a child, but left too quickly to understand.

For the past several years, I have been in practice as a psychologist and hypnotherapist. I have often listened to patients express dissatisfaction with themselves and their relationships. They have been especially disappointed and frustrated with their sexual and romantic relationships. I have watched them struggle with loneliness, depression, co-dependency and low self-esteem. I have helped them to communicate more effectively, achieve more intimacy and feel better about themselves. During the therapeutic process, each of my patients has taught me about life and relationships in unique and wonderful ways. One of the most important things that I have learned is that we are all striving for deeper intimacy and lingering ecstasy.

In my work as a hypnotherapist, I have observed the expansion of consciousness and the occurrence of amazing phenomena. Sometimes hypnosis has dramatically shown me the power of the human mind and left me breathless with excitement. For many years, I tended to remain skeptical about hypnosis, often discounting events in the name of science. For example, I refused to help individuals do past life regressions because I was concerned about the lack of scientific verification. In spite of my skepticism, hypnotherapy has been a delightful adventure leading me into the mystical parts of my inner self. With hypnosis, I have been given new and different perspectives that I never knew existed in the world, much less inside of myself.

And I have learned that the expansion of the mind is indeed limitless.

A few years ago, several different friends and colleagues began to tell me about some personal experiences which were unusual and highly spiritual. Some of their reports seemed irrational to me at the time, but I had difficulty discounting them because I knew and respected these individuals. They were intelligent, well-educated, conservative, competent people (physicians, engineers, psychologists, accountants, teachers) who tended to be analytical and even scientific. None of them belonged to any strange groups or described themselves as metaphysically oriented. Most of them did not know or associate with each other. They shared with me quietly as friends, expressing concern that many people would not understand their spiritual experiences. I remembered having similar experiences as a child and recalled the lingering feelings of ecstasy. In my private thoughts, I wondered if I could re-create these states of rapture as an adult.

Regardless of the above events, this book would never have been born if I had not met my beloved friend and co-author, Grant Bingeman. His creative insight, skillful writing, consistent encouragement and childlike faith enabled me to make a commitment to the creation of *Limitless Intimacy*. I recall saying quite flippantly, "We should write a book about this." Grant replied simply, "Let's do it." Then I confided that I had always wanted to write a book by recording tapes and having someone transcribe them for me. During the next week Grant repeatedly asked, "When are you going to give me a tape?" Soon I was recording tapes and we were writing a book.

In a very dramatic way *Limitless Intimacy* wrote itself, leading me through vast streams of ideas that I neither anticipated nor knew I possessed. There were many days that my writing began at one place and ended at a different place which I had never consciously considered. Sometimes the stream of ideas was too rapid for writing and I could capture them only on tape. Sometimes I would be unaware of what I had said or forget some of the information that I had recorded. However, writing this book was not simply an ethereal flight of ideas, but also an education in itself and a tremendous amount of work. I still do not understand the creative process, but I do know that it is by experience and shared experience that I have learned the most important concepts presented in *Limitless Intimacy*.

I still consider myself a scientist, but feel that I am an artistic, creative scientist. I know that I am now more enlightened and spiritually centered. Occasionally, I have conflicts between my creative and analytic processes. The analytical part of my brain has told me that some readers will dislike the language used in this book and object to terms such as altered states of consciousness, out-of-body experiences and spiritual sex. At one point, I wanted to substitute words that sounded more scientific (such as non-local mind, expanded awareness, beyond-the-brain, quantum mind, etc.) for some of the terms used in this book. Of course, I would have simply been playing a word game if I had substituted terms. I have discovered, again and again, that words are inadequate attempts to describe the experience of limitless intimacy.

Even though words are inadequate, I wanted to share the dynamic experiences presented in this book. I have experienced the ecstasy. Other people have shared the ecstasy. Our experiences are alive and real. I did not want to just tell the reader about spirituality and sexuality. I wanted each individual to really know through experience. The creation of this book is my attempt to help the reader experience deep intimacy and lingering ecstasy. My dream is for all of us to live in limitless intimacy. To each one who reads this book, "I wish you the rapture of spiritual sex and the bliss of limitless intimacy."

Narecia Hamrick, Ph.D.

Notes From Grant:

How do you describe something which is indescribable? That was my biggest challenge in writing this book. When we consider that the simplest emotion can only be understood by direct experience, how could I ever attempt to communicate the expanded state of awareness we call *limitless intimacy*. Yet I felt compelled to try, because I know that an abstract idea can grow to become experientially, personally real. All it takes is a little acceptance.

Perhaps you are one of the lucky ones who has had a spontaneous mystical experience, or who can fly in a lucid dream whenever you wish, or do some very real things that most people would label a fantasy. Those of you who know, know. And for those of you who aren't sure about some altered states because you may not have experienced them yet yourself, may I suggest that when you read the personal accounts in *Limitless Intimacy,* you recognize that the people who spoke the words were feeling something very strongly. Their experiences were very real to them. In fact there are physical effects that accompany the altered states — effects such as expanded pupils, changes in pulse and breathing, etc. So keep in mind that the "high" of limitless intimacy is not just emotional, spiritual and mental — it is also physical.

Many spiritual experiences are very personal, and sometimes very intense and powerful. For example, I can recall one from twenty years ago as if it were yesterday. Here is a transcription of an attempt I once made to share my experience.

> *I lost my sense of time, and I could see all things simultaneously. I could see past, present and future at the same time. I knew where I was, and yet I was more than there and then, I was everywhere and everywhen. All events were*

simultaneous. And there was a presence, a sentient presence that was kind of . . . I don't know, it's just completely beyond words.

Anyway, there was this presence that said, more or less, "Look at this." So I saw, and it didn't matter if my eyes were open or closed. I saw a point, a place where "evolution" or time had brought everything to. It was where homo-sapiens — that's what we call ourselves, Cro-Magnon man or whatever — no longer existed, but was just something way back in the chain.

The place was like a very complicated city . . . a myriad of individual people who existed completely, totally connected to each other — not cut off in any way — distinct and separate, but totally part of each and every other sentience. It was like a social structure you might say, but where nothing ever fought anything else because everyone knew what everyone else was doing. There was no conflict. Everybody knew where the flow was, which was on more levels and dimensions than we normally consider, by the way.

So, there could be this incredible concentration of intelligences in a very tight space, and some pretty big projects could get done. And there was no discord, but there was individual activity. I could see the facets of the structure and the whole at the same time. And I could see when it was occurring in, you might say, logarithmic scale or some other non-linear yardstick, but not time as we perceive it here.

The timescape was so very clear in that special state where I was, and yet it does not translate into our normal concept of days and years. It was a way of knowing I had never experienced before. You know how you can get a better view from a higher vantage point? Well, the view I had was from all vantage points at once, inside, outside, before, after, and something more. It's the "more" that really gets lost in the *translation. There were some things I saw that I understood then, but I simply do not have the referents for now.*

So I can't say that this community of limitless intimacy exists 30,000 years from now, because it really exists now. And it's nice to know that it's there, the future-now, because it gives me a real sense of purpose in that I know that I'm this step in evolution (or God's plan, whatever you want to call it, it doesn't matter). I'm right here and because I'm right here, these meta-people are going to be here later, yet somehow they are already here. There is a real connectedness to it. The same holds true for all the generations that preceded me. And I think that's why I decided I would have children. I know that sounds vain somehow, but it's really a faith and a certainty that things will get better, incredibly better.

*The amazing thing is that what I saw is not the end-all, be-all of life and sentience. It is more like a beginning of the next stage. To see beyond that would really be something to look forward to. And I think that **will** happen, and it **has** happened, and it **is** happening.*

Thinking back on this experience, afterwards I didn't want to use the word "God" ever again, because my original concept of God now meant to me something that was such a shallow imitation of the reality and not even that. For a long time afterwards, whenever someone said the word "God" I kind of had to bite my tongue. I knew that there was a lot more, but it was nothing you could talk about.

I didn't speak about this experience to anyone for a long time, because I felt that it would cheapen the experience. I mean, it had to be experienced to be understood, and it was pointless to try to explain it to another person . . . unless the other person had experienced the same thing, but then explanations would be superfluous. So for a long time I kind of smiled to myself. And then I decided I should do something with it; I just didn't know what, until this book was conceived.

Actually, I have mixed feelings about placing this translation of my most treasured experience in the preface of this or any book, yet it seems to be related to the material in an inextricable way. Sharing this experience makes me feel vulnerable. But it's a misconception to consider limitless intimacy a personal or individual experience, just as it is a mistake to think of each person as separate and alone. So it's time to be honest. Wouldn't you like to live in a world where you could actually share your deepest feelings, and be free of the worry of hurting someone, or being hurt?

For those of you who have experienced the ecstasy, isn't it wonderful? For those of you who have forgotten, wasn't it wonderful when you felt it? Now if we could just live within it forever. And we can!

Grant Bingeman, P.E.

INTRODUCTION

Why are we here? Where are we going? These are spiritual questions about our existence and the meaning of life. We have become discouraged in our search for answers to these questions. We try to find meaning in our sexual and romantic relationships, yet many of us remain dissatisfied. We seek true intimacy and lingering ecstasy, but our search often seems futile. It appears that our whole society has a dismal track record in the area of interpersonal relationships. We have become disillusioned with sex and romance, so we doubt our ability to maintain intimacy and ecstasy. Sometimes we are even afraid or embarrassed to say that we yearn to share an intense lingering ecstasy with another person.

In our search for meaning, we have created an unnatural split between sexuality and spirituality, but sex and spirit are inherently intertwined and inseparable. It is time for us to recognize that we are spiritual beings living in a universe that runs on sexual energy. When we unify and balance our sexual and spiritual experiences, we will be able to share spiritual sex — the ultimate intimacy and ecstasy. What is spiritual sex? It is difficult to describe and has to be experienced to be fully understood. Can you imagine having an orgasm in every cell of your mind and body simultaneously? This is the magical realm of spiritual sex.

It is one thing to read about sexuality or spirituality, but it is quite another to experience the rapture of spiritual sex. This book has been designed to allow you to unite with your spiritual self and to create a new kind of intimacy with others. It is a fun book. It is fun to read and so pleasurable to experience. We had fantastic experiences doing the exercises and you will, too.

Many individuals have already shared these wonderful states of ecstasy. When we try to describe spiritual sex, words often seem inadequate, but the concepts presented in this book are vital and alive. The experiences are real. The transcripts presented throughout the book are verbatim reports from individuals who have expanded their consciousness into the spiritual realm or shared the ecstasy of spiritual sex. When you read the beautiful reports of spiritual sex, you will find your heart beating with anticipation, your mind drifting into the ecstasy, and your body tingling with excitement.

Spiritual sex is a pathway to the creation of limitless intimacy. As spiritual beings, we are filled with divine sexual energy and have limitless potential for ecstasy. Simply by expanding awareness, we begin to love ourselves and others unconditionally. With spiritual sex, we are propelled into the divine state of limitless intimacy and share ecstasy beyond belief. Sex and spirit then become united and we have a direct, perfect and instantaneous communication of our deepest feelings and thoughts. Would you like to experience a form of understanding that goes beyond words and thoughts into a direct knowing of the very essence of your special lover? You can learn to share in this wonderful way by simply doing the exercises in this book.

Why are we here? Where are we going? The answers to these questions have many facets; but ultimately, when we understand one key concept, everything else fits into place. And this key concept is simply that we are not separate, we are not apart, we are not alone even though we feel scared and lost much of the time. What we really are is the sun and the moon and the stars, the wind in the trees, the tears in each other's eyes, and so much more.

We get to this special state of limitless intimacy when we share the ecstasy of spiritual sex.

1

SAWNKI

The Search

Sex As We Now Know It (SAWNKI) can be very good; it is a path to ecstasy. But we often have a nagging feeling that it could be better. Even the very best sexual experience leaves something to be desired, if only because we ask ourselves, "Why can't it be like this all the time?"

We often feel a vague dissatisfaction, a sense of something missing, a desire to be totally lost in the moment and a longing for more. Many of us are searching for a deeper intimacy and a lingering ecstasy which the body cannot totally provide. We want an intense, pleasurable feeling that will last, but the body only gives us temporary satisfaction. So we continue to yearn for love, intimacy and lingering ecstasy.

Perhaps we have become anesthetized to ecstasy, forgotten how to play or become too busy to share intimately. It seems that we have lost what once came naturally; we have lost skills which allowed us to live with the excitement, anticipation, exuberance and keen curiosity of a child. It is as though we have become numb to the joy of life.

A source of difficulty for many of us is the assumption that what we lack is somewhere "out there," and we have to go out into the unknown to find it. We search aimlessly for an unknown "something." Because our search seems so futile, we often become disenchanted or angry with ourselves and others. So we may discard relationships carelessly or cling to them desperately. As we become more dissatisfied, our yearning increases and we grasp objects or activities in a misguided effort to find relief. We often develop addictions to drugs, alcohol, relationships, work, exercise, cigarettes and food. When one addiction fails to satisfy us, we simply trade it for another. We are like angry children thrashing about in our playpens trying to find a new toy to make us happy.

Why do we make things so difficult? We make things difficult because we have been taught that we can't have everything, that we have to deserve happiness before getting happiness, that love is painful, that we must sacrifice or struggle and a hundred other self-limiting beliefs. But the simple truth is that we can have it all, right now, if we choose. Everything we need is already part of us. All we have to do is accept it. And the most amazing revelation is that we have already begun to embrace the truth.

Intimacy and Freedom

There is a human cry for more intimacy, more touching, more sharing, more closeness. We want desperately to feel love and to know that we are loved. And we all seek a special bond with another human. As souls developing human form in our mothers' uteruses, we were automatically, intensely bonded to our mothers. Following birth, we bonded with other individuals through nurturing and contact comfort. All these bonds contained a pure, innocent and natural element of sexual pleasure, but these were bonds with total dependency and no freedom.

As we matured into separate individuals, we gained freedom and lost intimacy. That most pleasurable infant bond of being in the womb of another was lost forever when we were born. As we grew up, we enjoyed our freedom but we often felt lonely, even abandoned. As adults, we continue to search for our lost intimacy and to seek ways of returning to the pleasure of that early bonding.

Some of our activities are particularly enjoyable, because they simulate a return to the womb or evoke unconscious infantile memories. Consider the joy of sex in a hot-tub, swimming pool or shower. Savor the memory of sensuous movements in a water-bed. Recall the delight of kissing and remember that babies experience an innocent form of sexual pleasure when they nurse. All these activities are wonderful, but they cannot replace the intimacy of the womb, so we continue to feel lonely.

Our loneliness motivates us to move closer to other people. But as we develop more intimacy, we tend to lose freedom. Our loss of freedom motivates us to move away from others. We have learned to cherish our freedom, yet yearn to recapture that infant bond of intimacy. Generally, we vacillate between moving closer to others and moving farther away from them.

Pleasure and Orgasm

When we express our sexuality in a positive way, we are reminded of the intense pleasure and comfort of the womb. Yet this memory stimulates a pervasive sense of loss and incompleteness. We long for more pleasure and deeper intimacy. So is born our search for a more intensely satisfying sexual experience, a search for that elusive bigger and better "O."

A friend once told us that her idea of heaven was a continual orgasm. As nice as this may seem, it is still limited thinking, because there is a step beyond orgasm to something truly incredible — something we have to experience to understand, because words simply fail to convey the reality.

Do you think you could tell a non-orgasmic woman what it feels like to have an orgasm? Of course you could tell her and she could repeat your words, but do you think she would really understand? No, the only way for her to fully comprehend an orgasm is to experience one.

Now take a quantum leap, and imagine what it would feel like to experience something that compares to orgasm like the taste of ice-water compares to dust. It staggers our imagination, doesn't it? Fortunately, there is no need to describe this state, if we can show you how to achieve it on your own. And we can. And you can.

A Joyful Reminiscence

The following exercise is designed to help you recall a recent peak sexual experience — one of those delicious moments which we all yearn to relive again and again. This experience begins with a simple relaxation exercise and concludes with a vivid recall of an intense sexual event that occurred during your recent sexual history.

You will begin by learning to recognize the difference between tension and relaxation. As adults we have spent many years learning how to be tense. Numerous stresses and demands have caused us to be uptight. And now we want to create relaxation. Relaxation, like tension, is a learned response. Relaxation was natural for us as children, but as adults we have learned to be tense. Fortunately, it is impossible to be tense and relaxed at the same time. So this exercise will teach you how to relax and to recognize deep muscle relaxation.

Read the entire exercise over once, silently to yourself. Then go back and read each part out loud, pausing after each section for a moment of reflection. Then put the book aside, make yourself very comfortable, do the relaxation exercise and recall that wonderful adult sexual event. It is not necessary to follow the dialogue precisely. Just tense and relax different parts of your body until your whole body is relaxed. Then let the recall of your sexual event evolve naturally and easily. If you wish to use a tape for this exercise, please consult the appendix for instructions on recording your own tape. You may prefer to order professionally recorded tapes from the publisher. In any case, let everything that you recall be positive and beneficial.

Lie down, position your body comfortably and just focus on developing relaxed feelings throughout your body. Allow yourself to relax. Now clench both your fists very tightly. Clench them tighter and tighter. Keep your fists clenched and feel the tension. Feel the tension in your hands, wrists and forearms. Become aware of how uncomfortable it feels.

Now relax. Let the fingers of your hands become loose and open. Let the muscles relax all the way up your arms to your shoulders. Enjoy this pleasant feeling. Become aware of the soothing, delightful relaxation.

Allow your entire body to become relaxed — completely, deeply relaxed. This is the opposite of tension. Your whole body becomes looser and more relaxed as you become aware, focusing on the looseness and limpness. Pause for a moment to really enjoy this feeling.

Now tense up again. Pull your shoulders up and try to touch your head. Feel the tension in your neck and shoulders. Become aware of the uncomfortable tightness. Hold this position for a moment.

Drop your shoulders and relax. Appreciate and enjoy the relief. Allow your shoulders, your neck, your back and chest to relax completely. Let the relaxation flow, flowing down into your neck and across your shoulders, into your arms and chest. Pause and let your entire body relax and enjoy this soothing feeling of relaxation.

Now direct your attention to your facial muscles. Wrinkle up your forehead. Frown and crease your brow. Clench your jaws and bite your teeth together firmly. Press your tongue to the roof of your mouth. Feel all the uncomfortable tension in your face, jaws, forehead and cheeks.

Relax and enjoy. It's such a relief to relax, such a contrast. You can feel the relaxation spreading all the way up your scalp to the top of your head, then back down to your shoulders. Breathe easily and freely. Take an extra moment now to enjoy that feeling of relaxation.

Focus your attention on your stomach muscles. Make your stomach tense by tightening your stomach and drawing the muscles in. Hold this tension and feel the discomfort. Then push your stomach out and feel this contrasting tension. Again, tighten your stomach muscles, drawing them in tighter and tighter.

Let go and relax, freely, easily. Breathe gently and easily. Let your stomach muscles relax more and more, deeper and deeper. All the tension is dissolving now. It is like the difference between iron and pudding — relaxed, limp, loose. Pause and enjoy this feeling of relaxation.

Tense the lower part of your body. Point your toes toward your face, and make the muscles in your legs hard and tight with tension. Become aware of the tension. Feel it. Then point your toes away from your face and tighten your legs. Tighten your muscles all the way up your legs to your hips. Become aware of this tightness and tension.

Now relax and enjoy. It feels so good. Feel the relaxation in your feet spreading into your calves and knees, thighs and hips. Let go more and more. Feel the relaxation in your stomach and waist, your lower and upper back, your shoulders, chest and neck. Keep relaxing more and more. Relax all the way down to the tips of your fingers, and all the way up to the top of your head. Relax, deeper and deeper.

As you lie there comfortably, you relax more and more. Continue to let go. With each free, gentle and easy breath you take, you experience a deeper, more enjoyable relaxation. It is like years of tension and stress are vanishing.

Let the pleasure of this feeling of relaxation spread throughout your body. The relaxation becomes pleasure — so pleasurable. As you savor this wonderful feeling, you will automatically begin to return to a delightful sexual experience. You will recall an adult experience, an experience which occurred after you reached full maturity and awareness.

Begin by remembering, by visualizing the events and feelings that led up to that wonderful, delightful experience. Recall the excited anticipation. Become aware of what you were thinking and the feelings that began to build almost immediately. Remember your surroundings, the smells and sounds, the touching and physical sensations. Recall the way that your body seemed to vary from excited tension to smooth velvet — the stroking, pounding, and drifting.

Experience and enjoy the memory of the thrusting, vibrating, increasing arousal that seemed to spread from your toes to the top of your head. Visualize the caressing, stroking and touching. Re-experience the longing for more and more and more. Perhaps you experienced kissing again and again, or hugging, petting, and dancing. Whatever experiences, sensations, feelings that you had . . . recall them vividly in detail, relishing each and every moment. Become aware of the increase in your heartbeat and respiration, the flow, the kind-of passionate waves of pleasure flowing throughout your body.

If your peak sexual experience included orgasm, recall that building pleasure-energy, the tingling sensation, the erection in your nipples. Only the pleasure exists at some point and everything else fades into the background. All that exists is pleasure, waves and waves of pleasure that burst into an explosion of energy and ecstasy. Time and space cease to exist as you experience contraction after contraction, an explosive orgasm. Waves of pleasure burst forth and spread throughout every cell and atom of your body. Cold chills spread across your thighs and your chest all the way down into your toes — flowing outward from your genitals. Pleasure envelops every part of your body, until the old reality ceases to exist and only waves and waves of pleasure remain.

Allow yourself the joy of this lingering experience and become aware of how you felt afterwards. Recall the inner feelings of peace, relaxation and tranquility. Recapture that indescribable, delicious pleasure that lingers and lingers. Recall the feelings and experiences that occurred after your peak sexual event.

When you recall this peak sexual event, begin by getting in touch with the feelings, activities and experiences that led up to the special interaction. Remember the delicious details of the event itself. Be sure to get in touch with the feelings inside your body; within your genitals, the erection or the tingling and throbbing in your vagina. Re-experience all the delicious details — the lights, colors, sounds, feelings inside and on the surface of your body. Let the feelings radiate throughout your entire body. Then recall the positive feelings and experiences that followed your special sexual event.

Slowly savoring it all, go back and recall the beginning, the anticipation and the building of your climax. Re-experience that delightful, explosive, indescribable orgasm. Savor the pleasure and events after your orgasm — that wonderful climax that lingered and lingered and continues to linger forever.

A Glorious Evolution

Let's consider the glorious evolution of SAWNKI. What changes in sexual customs have occurred during your lifetime? Can you imagine what sex was like 100 years ago? Certainly it was distorted and limited by superstition and ignorance. Think of the wonderful journey that our ancestors have made, and how lucky we are to be living in a time of increased sexual awareness.

Recently, we asked an elderly woman if she recalled any superstitious methods of birth control from her youth. "Oh, no," she replied, "Sex was a shameful thing that no one ever discussed!" Yet this woman has now received a letter from the Surgeon General of the United States which discusses the explicit use of condoms. This same letter was mailed to every household of record in the U.S. in 1988. What a remarkable change in just this woman's lifetime!

Ask your parents, grandparents or some elderly individuals about sexual customs they recall from their youth. You will be amused and amazed by what you learn. For example, a grandmother told us that women would try to hide their pregnancies and would not leave the house until they just "suddenly had a baby." Even more amazing, she reported that mothers would continue to nurse their children in secret (hiding behind doors and in closets) until the children were five or six years old, because the mothers believed they could not become pregnant as long as they were nursing.

Here is an excerpt from a book published in 1903 titled *The Perfect Woman*. We feel that not everyone who lived back then adhered to these tenets, but some individuals probably took them quite seriously.

> *I say to you, mother, and oh, so ernestly: "Go teach your boy that which you may never be ashamed to do, about these organs that make him specially a boy."*
>
> *Teach him they are called sexual organs, that they are not impure, but of special importance, and made by God for a definite purpose.*
>
> *Impress upon him that if these organs are abused, or if they are put to any use besides that for which God made them—and He did not intend they should be used at all until man is fully grown—they will bring disease and ruin upon those who abuse and disobey those laws which God has made to govern them.*
>
> *If he has ever learned to handle his sexual organs, or to touch them in any way except to keep them clean, not to do it again. If he does, he will not grow up happy, healthy and strong.*
>
> *Teach him that when he handles or excites the sexual organs, all parts of the body suffer, because they are connected by nerves that run throughout the system, this is why it is called "self-abuse." The whole body is abused when this part of the body is handled or excited in any manner whatever.*
>
> *Teach them to shun all children who indulge in this loathsome habit or all children who talk about these things. The sin is terrible, and is, in fact, worse than lying or stealing! For, although these are wicked and will ruin their soul, yet this habit of self-abuse will ruin both soul and body.*

If the sexual organs are handled it brings too much blood to these parts, and this produces a diseased condition; it also causes disease in other organs of the body, because they are left with a less amount of blood than they ought to have. The sexual organs, too, are very closely connected with the spine and the brain by means of the nerves, and if they are handled, or if you keep thinking about them, these nerves get excited and become exhausted, and this makes the back ache, the brain heavy and the whole body weak.

It lays the foundation for consumption, paralysis and heart disease. It weakens the memory, makes a boy careless, negligent and listless.

It even makes many lose their minds; others, when grown, commit suicide.

How often mothers see their little boys handling themselves, and let it pass, because they think the boy will outgrow the habit, and do not realize the strong hold it has upon them! I say to you, who love your boys—"Watch!"

Don't think it does no harm to your boy because he does not suffer now, for the effects of this vice come on so slowly that the victim is often very near death before you realize that he has done himself harm.

The boy with no knowledge of the consequences, and with no one to warn him, finds momentary pleasure in its practice, and so contracts a habit which grows upon him, undermining his health, poisoning his mind, arresting his development, and laying the foundation for future misery.

These amazing attitudes were present in the literature over a span of several decades around the turn of the century. Surely, many of our ancestors were misinformed and repressed. We have come such a long way; thank goodness those who lived before us did a lot of the work! They obviously had much to overcome.

Reflection on our wonderful evolutionary journey of SAWNKI gives cause for laughter and celebration. Each of us may also be pleased with our individual contributions to this wonderful trip. We have truly come a long way. Our attitudes toward sex have shown a healthful trend toward understanding and acceptance in recent decades. Perhaps you can remember when "French" kissing, flirting, oral sex and unusual positions for intercourse were much less acceptable than they are today. Our attitudes have certainly become more positive and accepting.

An Adolescent Delight

Here is a simple imagery exercise which will help you reflect on an important part of your personal evolution. It begins with the relaxing image of a boat trip and concludes with the vivid memory of an intense sexual event that occurred during your adolescence. This event may be as simple as a kiss.

Refer to the appendix to order professionally recorded tapes from the publisher, or follow the instructions given in the appendix to record your own tape for this exercise. When your tape is ready, make yourself comfortable, visualize the boat trip, recall those teen years and remember that intense sexual event. Let it evolve naturally and easily as you relax. And let everything that you recall be positive and beneficial.

> Begin by closing your eyes and positioning your body comfortably. Slow your breathing and allow your muscles to become loose and limp. Then imagine that you are sitting in a very comfortable lounge chair aboard a large riverboat. The boat is floating slowly down a beautiful part of the Mississippi River. The temperature is perfect on this beautiful spring day.

You enjoy the warmth of the sun and the motion of the boat as it creates a gentle breeze. Watch the water as it ripples along the side of the boat and glistens in the sun. Listen to the rhythmic splashing sound of the water. As the boat moves farther and farther down the river, you relax more and more. Each muscle loosens and relaxes.

Imagine this relaxing vacation. It is such a beautiful trip. Look along the banks of the river and observe the large trees covered with moss draping softly toward the water. See the colorful birds fly from the trees, glide upward, then disappear again within the trees. You are fascinated by the artistic illusions — lush green trees against a clear blue sky, grey moss hanging in shadow, sunlight sparkling across the water.

You become aware of quaint river houses and fantasize about the days of Huckleberry Finn. Occasionally a fish jumps out of the water leaving a cascade of iridescent droplets suspended in the air. You pass old wooden piers with interesting people fishing. And you hear conversations in the distance, but can't quite make out the words.

Continue to imagine drifting and floating down the river until you are completely relaxed. Then allow yourself to recall — remembering clearly and vividly — a very special adolescent sexual experience that occurred with another person. It could have started with a touch, a look, a kiss, a fantasy, a special song, a dance, a fun activity or in a hundred different ways.

Begin by taking a moment to see yourself as a joyful teenager. Recall positive experiences and only positive experiences. Remember the exuberance and enthusiasm of youth. Recall those youthful characteristics — the eagerness, boldness, shyness, confusion and boundless energy.

There was a kind of freshness in the air, a blushing newness all around you. Visualize the clothes and hairstyles of adolescence. Recall that special teen language and the unique mannerisms. It's fun just to remember this special period of youth, its excitement and boundless energy. Listen and smile as you recall the music, the sports and unique activities of those teenage years. Recall only positive, happy images. Experience the sounds, colors and movements which create flowing pictures of teenagers, places and events.

Your relationships during these teen years had a fresh, exciting quality about them. And your body responded to this excitement. Remember those delightful sexual changes that occurred in your body as you moved toward adulthood. Recall your awareness of the growth of pubic hair or the development of breasts, the deepening of your voice or the development of your genitals. You and your peers were all experiencing a variety of body changes, similar in many ways, but also unique to each individual. These wonderful changes brought forth adult development, adult sexual functioning. The unique changes in your body were new, exciting, wonderful and at times scary.

When you have recalled some positive images of those teenage years, then begin to remember a special sexual event. Create positive images of those intense sexual feelings. Recall the delicious pleasure you experienced while interacting with someone special — that very intense sexual moment. It was an event that awakened your new adult sexuality. Perhaps it began with a special touch, a look across the room, a hug, a kiss, a dance, a daydream or in some other way. You may have felt cold chills, weak knees, and changes in your breathing or heart-rate. Remember those wonderful feelings in your genitals, perhaps a delightful tingling and throbbing in your vagina, or an intense, automatic erection of your penis.

Get in touch with the feelings and experiences that led up to your special sexual interaction. Recall the delicious details of the event itself. And then remember the positive feelings and experiences which followed your unique sexual event. Take a few minutes to savor all the positive feelings, thoughts, perceptions and behaviors associated with your special adolescent sexual interaction.

When you are ready to end the exercise, let yourself count out loud, counting slowly, from one to ten. Allow yourself to become more alert and energetic with each count.

Limitations and Inhibitions

Are you proud of your sexual growth, but still feel limited or vaguely dissatisfied? Do you yearn for increased intimacy, greater ecstasy and complete freedom? You are not alone. The simple fact is that SAWNKI has built-in limitations which inhibit our pleasure and foster loneliness and distance.

SAWNKI is sometimes limited by our institutions which may attempt to regulate sex. Our churches for example, seem to have helped create an artificial separation between what we define as physical and what we define as spiritual. This of-the-body and of-the-spirit separation also has connotations of "bad" and "good." Because sex is of the body and therefore "bad," it is often repressed so that it pops up in hurtful or exploitable ways. Our doctrines have sometimes suggested that sex is no more than animal lust unless first transformed by proprietary rituals. And we have sometimes forbidden recreational sex, while sanctioning procreational sex. Fortunately, we are now recognizing these artificial separations, developing healthful attitudes toward sex and a holistic philosophy about the body.

Fear is our great limiter, affecting most of us both consciously and unconsciously. Some of our common sexual fears include: disease, punishment, pregnancy, performance, rejection, vulnerability and obligation. Our fears may be related to cultural, religious and societal prohibitions. Of course, we understand that societal prohibitions vary from culture to culture and generation to generation. We also know that some of our fears are silly and irrational. But even when we understand our fears, they may be quite difficult for us to overcome.

Through fear and superstition, we have often inhibited and blocked the power of our own sexuality and kept ourselves ignorant of the truth. Let us freely embrace our sexual spirituality in affirmation of wholeness and goodness. We can accept what is natural and know that it is right. Let us accept our sexuality as a wonderful gift. When you give a gift to someone, how do you want them to feel?

Let's just cast aside our inhibitions and enjoy SAWNKI! Sometimes this is easily done and we are able to have a "peak" experience. But have you ever felt sexually inhibited, especially at that precise moment when you wanted most to be free and responsive? If only there were a way! And there is! We can learn to share freely and completely the very essence of ourselves, when we become open to the ecstasy of spiritual bonding.

Laughter can be a key for us, opening the door to acceptance and affirmation. Do you ever laugh at your own negativity? Perhaps you alternately laugh and lament? Our comedies, cartoons and jokes often target sexual behaviors and beliefs. And while comedy helps us to relax and avoid taking ourselves too seriously, it also reminds us of the undercurrent of negativity within SAWNKI. Many of us have been taught that sex is dirty, bad, shameful, immoral, degrading, sinful and disgusting. In this context, we have learned that sex creates anxiety, guilt, danger, trouble, complexity and irreversible change, not to mention zits!

An acquaintance told us a funny story of his first time in bed with a willing girl. He was seventeen, a high school football player. His parents had just bought him a water bed which he was anxious to try out. They were gone for the weekend, so he was alone with his girlfriend and everything seemed perfect. His girlfriend was lying naked on the bed. In his eagerness, he leaped onto the water bed, but the huge wave he created immediately threw him out onto the floor. His girlfriend burst into hysterical laughter, and the experience inhibited the poor fellow for years afterwards.

Here is another amusing anecdote. A man shared an apartment with his sister. It was not often that he had the apartment to himself, so when he finally had an evening alone with his latest flame, he created a very romantic setting for her with dinner, wine, candles, music and flowers. At the moment they were headed for the bedroom, his cat came to the back door. As he attempted to let the cat in, he broke a pane in the door, severing an artery. The girl rushed him to the hospital, but the experience created a vague worry which distracted them during all their subsequent sexual relations together.

Maybe these experiences are unusual, but most of us have learned at least a few inhibitions that detract from the enjoyment of sex, and some of us cannot perform at all under very ordinary circumstances. Perhaps we are distracted when the lights are on, or when the kids are awake, or when our eyes are open, or if our partner wants to try something new, or if our partner is too noisy, or if we are not under the covers, or if we have not first had a few drinks and so on.

How often do you distract yourself by worrying about sexual performance? When we are monitoring and analyzing, instead of letting go, sex becomes a calculated, mechanical act. Good sex requires that we turn off our left brains and turn on our right brains where dwell creativity, intuition, emotion, imaging, instinct, sensory perception, and an altered state of consciousness that embraces the big picture.

Our left brains are verbal, logical, analytical and temporal (keeping track of time). They cannot think in pictures and metaphors. They are not creative, so they lack inspiration and insight. Our left brains are simply tools like computers are tools. They are very useful, but only meet part of our needs. If we choose to experience life mostly through our left brains, then we miss much of life. Isn't it better to dance than to watch the dancers? After all, the dancers use all of their brains, so experience life more fully.

Our limitations and inhibitions are learned behaviors. As small children, we had fewer inhibitions and still experienced much of life in our right brains. Because of our active right brains, many of us experienceed sexual pleasure in naturally uninhibited ways when we were very young. A friend told us of her first orgasm, which she experienced at five years of age. A new kid on the block surprised her with a forceful kiss on the lips, her first "real" kiss. She had an instant orgasm and it was wonderful. She said that she didn't know what it was at the time, but it sure beat the hell out of anything she had felt up to then. Wouldn't it be nice if we could enjoy an orgasm just from a kiss? Well, we can when we return to the child within.

Journey Back to Childhood

Here is a fun exercise which can help you return to an early childhood experience of sexual pleasure. Read the entire exercise silently to yourself, then make a tape following the instructions in the appendix or order professional tapes from the publisher. Let everything that you recall be positive and beneficial.

Begin this exercise by stretching out, perhaps with a pillow or blanket; cuddle up and become comfortable. Allow yourself to experience that perfect sense of warmth (or coolness) and that snuggly feeling, like a little child might snuggle up with a blanket or teddy bear.

Just take a deep breath and let every part of your body relax automatically. Relax deeper and deeper and begin to see waves of colors. Beautiful bright colors are fading in and out — gentle, soft colors. Let a kind of sleepiness spread throughout your mind and body. You feel so peaceful, with a wonderful kind of childlike freeness.

Relax deeper and deeper with each slow and gentle and free breath that you take. Within you is a wonderful carefree child — a child that has experienced the joy of relaxing and sleeping in the most peaceful, delightful way. Inside there is a child without responsibilities, a free and open child who is perceptually aware and amazed by everything. This child enjoys so much and experiences everything with freedom and delight. Get in touch with this little child inside of you now. Let the little child come out to play.

Visualize yourself as a little child, perhaps swinging in a swing set; swinging to and fro, back and forth, up and down. Perhaps you are also blowing bubbles and watching them drift in the wind. See the colors in the bubbles, iridescent colors. See translucent bubbles in the wind, with each free and easy and gentle breath you take . . . bubbles floating in the wind, bursting beautiful bubbles.

Now visualize yourself walking barefoot in the cool, thick grass. It feels so good pushing between your toes, soft but firm and springy. You can almost feel each individual shoot as it supports and massages the soles of your feet. See yourself lying on the grass and rolling over and over, looking upward at the leaves of the trees, and watching the clouds in the sky. Watch the clouds drifting lazily by. Visualize yourself wading a creek; feel that cool water, the smooth, clean stones. Hear the playful, bubbling, musical sounds. Listen to the sounds of young children playing in a wading pool, splashing and laughing.

Now see yourself as a little child rocking as though you were in a cradle or held in someone's arms, swaying back and forth, warm and secure, wrapped in a blanket, snuggly close, intimate, soft and secure. Enjoy that wonderful little child's sleep.

Now return to that most pleasurable experience, that sexual feeling when you were very young, when you were just a little child. Let the little child within return to that first ecstasy, that first sexual feeling. The feeling may have started with a touch, an embrace, an image, or perhaps music. It may have started in a thousand different ways, but you experienced it in your own personal way. Allow yourself to recall that feeling now, that feeling of strong sexual pleasure that began in some way unique to you and spread into your genitals. You knew that it was a wonderful feeling and a different feeling from any you had ever had before. It was a new, exciting and unique feeling of intense pleasure.

Remember that wonderful genital feeling. Enjoy the ease and freedom, the child's spontaneity and automatic perception of pleasure. It's so easy, so wonderful. Remember that wonderful first sexual feeling. Become aware of how natural, spontaneous, free and easy it was.

Remember the details, colors, sounds and feelings. See the objects or people. Recall the way that you experienced it, what happened before you experienced it and how you felt afterwards. Take a few moments to relish the feelings and enjoy them. Recall what led up to the feelings, those tremendous first sexual feelings. A positive, delightful memory remains with you. Let yourself recall it sweetly and in vivid detail.

When you are ready to refocus your attention, become aware of your surroundings and how relaxed you feel. Then count slowly from one to ten, telling yourself to become more energetic and alert with each count.

Personal Reflections

After you have read this chapter and completed the exercises, let yourself pause for some quiet moments of reflection. Reflect on feelings and ideas which are important to you — perhaps love, intimacy, freedom, faith, sex, pleasure, individuality, peace and ecstasy. Then answer the following questions, responding quickly with the first thoughts that enter your mind.

1. What do you want?

2. How would you recognize it?

3. What would it feel like?

4. How could you stop yourself from getting it?

5. What if you got everything you want?

Our best sexual experiences are an integration of physical, emotional and spiritual elements. And there is a synthesis beyond these elements, where the whole is much greater than the sum of its parts — much, much greater. There exists a state of consciousness, of awareness, of being, that involves a merging of souls without loss of individuality or freedom. We could call this the ultimate intimacy. This is what we are all looking for, what we are all being drawn to, whether we know it or not. And at some level, we all know it.

Affirmations

Have you observed an increase in your sexual interest and desire while reading this chapter? Did you begin to enjoy SAWNKI more when you completed the exercises? As you continue to observe your increased sexual interest and heightened pleasure, you will know that you are already making significant progress toward a goal of more ecstasy and limitless intimacy.

The following affirmations will strongly reinforce the new information which you are already beginning to internalize. Copy and post them in a prominent place where you can easily read them several times a day. Or you may simply wish to read them from the book each evening before retiring.

1. I now rejoice with the understanding that sexuality and spirituality are inseparable.

2. I am free to express my divine sexuality.

3. The more I pleasure myself sexually, the more I am able to pleasure others.

4. My sexual ecstasy is limitless.

5. I celebrate my own personal sexual evolution.

6. I triumphantly cast aside unfounded fears and joyfully express my sexuality.

7. I eagerly let go of worry and inhibition, and savor all my sexual expressions.

8. I joyfully anticipate the merging of profound intimacy and total freedom.

9. My words and thoughts about sex are positive, beautiful images of my spirituality.

10. I affirm the union of sex and spirit in the continual creation of abundant life.

Selected Readings

Binswanger, Ludwig. *Being in the World: Selected Papers of Ludwig Binswanger*, Basic Books, New York, 1963.

Blum, Jeffrey. *Living With Spirit in a Material World*, Ballantine Books, New York, 1988.

Boland, K.T. *The Perfect Woman*, unknown publisher, 1903.

Boss, Medard. *Psychoanalysis and Daseinsanalysis*, Basic Books, New York, 1963.

Buzan, Tony. *Use Both Sides of Your Brain*, E.P. Dutton, New York, 1983.

Ewin, Dabney. "Left-right Brain Research: Practical Use in Hypnosis," *Dallas Society of Clinical Hypnotists Newsletter*, Nov,1988, vol 8(2), pp2-7.

Frankl, Viktor E. *Man's Search for Meaning*, Washington Square Press, New York, 1984.

Freud, Sigmund. *The Standard Edition of the Complete Psychological Works*, J. Strachey (ed), Hogarth Press, London, 1953-1964.

Fromm, Eric. *Escape From Freedom*, Holt, Rinnehart, & Winston, New York, 1941.

Gawain, Shakti. *Living in The Light*, Whatever Publishing, San Rafael, California, 1986.

Horney, Karen. *Our Inner Conflicts*, Norton Press, New York, 1945.

Peele, Stanton & Brodsky, Archie. *Love and Addiction*, NAL Penguin, Inc., New York, 1976.

May, Rolo. *Existential Psychology* (2nd ed), Random House, New York, 1969.

McCuen, William G. *The Bicameral Brain and Human Behavior*, Vantage Publishing, New York, 1986.

Ramsdale, David & Dorfman, Ellen. *Sexual Energy Ecstasy*, Peak Skill Publishing, Playa Del Rey, California, 1985.

Rogers, Carl R. *On Becoming a Person*, Houghton Mifflin, New York, 1961.

Rusbridger, Alan. *A Concise History of the Sex Manual*, Faber and Faber, London, 1986.

2

FLYING HIGH NATURALLY

The First Step

SAWNKI is a path to ecstasy. We have traveled down this path on a wonderful evolutionary journey. Still we have continued to yearn for deeper intimacy, greater ecstasy and more freedom. Sadly, we have limited ourselves by assuming that we can't have it all. The reality is that we can have it all. We can "get high" naturally and "fly free" easily. We are like little birds who have a natural ability to fly, yet we are afraid of falling. When we let go of fear, we can embrace ecstasy and the freedom of limitless intimacy. At this moment it is all waiting just above the treetops of our awareness.

We remember the first time we saw the moons of Jupiter. We were in our own backyard when we looked through a pair of binoculars at the brightest light in the sky; we were amazed to see four tiny moons racing around it. We had spent our lives in ignorance of a very beautiful experience, yet all that time the moons were just beyond the edge of our awareness. Just like the moons of Jupiter, true intimacy hovers near the edge of our peripheral vision. We can get in touch with this magic by simply expanding our perception.

The first step in embracing the ultimate intimacy is a reaffirmation of our own spirituality. Who are we? Is there a "me" and a "you" that is more than body, more than brain? Are we simply garbage to be cast in a pit when we die? Clearly there is a "me" and a "you" that is eternal, everlasting spirit. Where were we before our bodies were conceived? Did we exist? Will we continue to exist after our hearts stop beating? Yes, of course — we change, but we cannot die. What we call "death" is simply one of our many glorious transitions.

At a precise moment of sexual union, we began a miraculous, wonderful transition into the realm of this physical life, leaving for awhile our existence in spiritual paradise. The womb is a link to the paradise that we have mercifully forgotten. But sometimes we remember fragments, so is it any wonder that we have unconscious desires to return to the womb? Let us rejoice as we remember that sexuality and spirituality are inherently linked in a beautiful, swirling vortex of ecstasy — that timeless moment of sexual union when conception occurs. Were you aware that some women know they are pregnant the moment it happens?

Awareness and ASCs

Every delightful orgasm, every beautiful artistic creation, every great achievement begins with an idea in the mind. As spiritual entities, we have a mind with an awareness or consciousness, which is more than a brain. We tend to equate awareness with the brain, but awareness is not simply a physical bundle of nerve ganglia, synapses and hormones. The mind is not just a computer made of meat. The truth is that the mind is an ever-expanding circle of awareness. And as the universe expands, so do we.

Often we tend to think of our awareness as being located in our heads, because the brain and some of our physical senses are in the head. Yet there is no evidence that awareness or consciousness is in the brain, the body or any particular place. Awareness is non-physical; it is divinely spiritual and cannot be limited to any one place. Could it be that what we call mind exists in all places and times simultaneously?

To facilitate our understanding of this non-local nature of mind, Rupert Sheldrake compares the brain to a television. We can poke around in the brain or the television and change what we see and hear, but this does not mean that what we perceive originates exclusively in the brain or in the television. In actuality, the signal is everywhere. And the brain is not the seat of awareness, just as the television is not the source of its programming.

Many changes or fluctuations in our awareness occur spontaneously and naturally. Hypnotists often refer to these variations as altered states of consciousness or ASCs. Relaxation, sleep and dreaming are common ASCs which we all experience. Some ASCs, such as spiritual/religious experiences and sexual orgasms are very intense and pleasurable.

What interesting ASCs have you observed during this past week? While teaching a class, we had an opportunity to observe several fluctuations in awareness. On the front row, we watched an entranced young woman drawing hearts and repeatedly writing her boyfriend's initials in her notebook. In the back of the room, an athletic fellow was gazing out the window smiling mischievously. And a student positioned in the middle of the room was staring straight at us, eyes fixated, mind obviously drifting out into space.

Each and every day, we all experience many alterations or changes in awareness or consciousness. Have you ever had the experience of becoming aware that you have turned several pages in a book and read the sentences on each page, yet you could not remember anything that you had read? Or during an automobile trip, have you suddenly realized that you have driven through several towns, but you didn't remember them? Or have you ever been startled into a state where everything seemed to move in slow motion? These types of ASCs are so common that we may not even notice them until someone calls them to our attention.

Perhaps you have also experienced a type of simultaneous dual awareness. Have you ever been sleeping and heard the telephone ringing, yet you continued to sleep, maybe even dream? In this state of dual awareness, you may have thought "The phone is ringing, but I'm asleep and dreaming and I can choose to answer the phone or continue with my dream." If you experience this type of dual awareness, then you have a wonderful opportunity for learning to control and expand your ASCs.

Have you ever known something without knowing how you knew it, yet you felt a certainty about it? Most of us have experienced inexplicable "gut" feelings from time to time that were correct even though they were in conflict with our logical, rational thoughts. Perhaps we have only begun to acknowledge how wonderful our awareness really is!

We all experience many altered states of consciousness every day. They are not reserved for the saintly. All of us have the ability to evoke truly wonderful states of being whenever we wish — states almost beyond explanation. Already, you are beginning to notice your ASCs while they are happening. Next time you notice one, let yourself go as far as the experience takes you. Avoid clutching at the experience, just enjoy and let it flow.

When we expand our awareness, we can savor the joy of flying free — free from the restrictions of the brain and the body. In actuality, we can easily move our awareness anywhere we want to move it, and we can experience and perceive reality beyond the range of our five physical senses. Perhaps this is less a process of moving our awareness, than it is of simply concentrating on a particular place and time where our awareness already exists. To enjoy this ability, we need only believe in it and break the habit of thinking that our awareness is stuck in our heads.

While reading SAWNKI, you have easily and automatically shifted your awareness many times. Shifting awareness is like shifting sand in an hourglass. Just turn the focus and the shift occurs automatically. But unlike sand in an hourglass, awareness is not confined to a container; rather, it exists freely in space and time. The potential expansion of our awareness is indeed limitless.

Understanding OBEs

The out-of-body experience, or OBE, is a wonderful state of extended awareness, which we can all learn to create and direct naturally. Out-of-body experiences have been variously referred to as spirit travel, astral projection, ESP, traveling clairvoyance and so on. Perhaps this confusion of terms exists because there are several different types of OBEs. However, all OBEs include a projection or extension of awareness beyond the physical location of the body.

Have you projected your awareness out of your body? The out-of-body experience is a common activity, which is sometimes labeled incorrectly or forgotten by the projector. Even so, we estimate that more than twenty percent of the general population will acknowledge having had an OBE. But the fact is, we have all traveled out of our bodies and will make these delightful journeys again and again.

To simplify our understanding, it is helpful to separate OBEs into two broad categories. Naturally-occurring OBEs are spontaneous, automatic and effortless. They may be motivated by factors such as pleasure, curiosity, convenience, necessity, insight, spiritual enlightenment, healing, empathy and sexual bonding. In contrast, artificially or physically-induced OBEs occur as a result of an assault on the body and the brain. They are usually stimulated by pain, shock, trauma, intense fear, severe deprivation, oxygen starvation, drugs or anesthesia. Obviously, we all want to increase our skills in directing naturally-occurring OBEs instead of physically-induced OBEs.

Naturally-occurring OBEs are very pleasurable, normal human activities which always include an extension of awareness beyond the physical location of the body. They create a feeling of exhilaration and freedom — a "high" which lingers for days. But unlike artificial "highs" produced by drugs, these OBEs also create a calm, centered, relaxed and peaceful feeling for the participant. OBEs are true bridges to ecstasy, and we have a natural ability to cross these bridges.

Childhood OBEs

As small children, we still experience much of life in the right brain and enjoy natural, spontaneous OBEs. But by the age of three or four, we are already learning left brain concepts of logic, numbers and temporal time. Discussions of "magic" and out-of-body experiences are usually discouraged by our scientific society. We are also taught to be perfectionistic, cautious and fearful by well-intentioned adults. Of course, we need to develop our left-brains to function successfully in this physical world. It just seems so sad to realize that we have lost much of our innate right-brain joy and wonder in the name of analytic thinking.

When given permission and acceptance, young children will often report their OBEs by talking about "flying through walls," "doing cartwheels above the class in school," "jumping over buildings" or "running away from my body." OBEs tend to have a playful, joyful quality in children and may occur frequently. When we observe joyful, happy children with boundless energy and vitality, we may be seeing the positive effects of their OBEs. It may also be that childrens' natural behavior promotes OBE.

Let's remember that the tiny child is parent to the adult, and we have much to learn when we return to the child within. We sometimes long for the lost exuberance and joy of childhood, without realizing that nothing is lost or misplaced in Spiritual Mind. What seems lost can always be found again and again.

Here is a description of a typical childhood OBE as related to the authors by an individual who has recently begun to recall some of her early experiences. Note that this OBE occurred spontaneously, naturally and effortlessly.

I was at school and I remember there was always this undercurrent of — a lot of cliques. And there was a certain amount of competition and jealousy. I lived in a small town where, basically, everybody knew everybody. Not only did you know everyone in your class, you knew half the people in the school and half of the people in town. There were only about fifty students in my graduating class. I was eight years old, so that would have put me in about the third grade.

You can see why a new child who had just moved into town was unusual enough that everyone in the class would notice. And it would be a big topic of conversation. It was something different. So when a new child moved into town, that child might be very popular, at least for a while, because they were someone new.

This one particular morning, we had just started changing classes. One of my little girlfriends had stopped me in the hallway to tell me there was a new girl who had just started school. She emphasized how pretty she was and how she had long blond hair and all the boys liked her. I don't remember exactly what she said, but the feeling I got was that this was really serious competition. I was used to being a child star and was pretty outgoing. I was probably born a flirt and got worse as I got older. This child appeared quite a threat to me by the description of the little girl. I can remember feeling a tremendous urgency to check out this child. I wanted to look at her and I did not want to wait.

She was in a classroom across the hall from me, so as soon as I sat down in my chair, I simply left my body — just boom — no effort to it at all. I floated across the room through the wall right straight into that classroom and immediately hovered above this one child. I recall hovering over her head and really checking her out, looking at her and looking all around. I watched her and listened to what was going on and then the funniest thing happened. I suddenly — it was like some kind of knowledge came to me. It was more direct knowledge, like an awareness with humor. It seemed so funny, so ridiculously absurd that I was concerned about this child and all these things.

It is almost impossible to describe, but I knew something beyond what I was usually capable of understanding. While I was there out of my body, I had a direct line to a higher spiritual knowledge that gave me, for that amount of time, an unusual sense of knowing. I knew my jealousy was nothing. The whole thing was trivial and ridiculous, so it didn't matter how beautiful she was. It didn't even matter if she had all the boys. I don't know exactly how to explain it, but it was very humorous. It made me laugh at myself in a joyful, happy way. Then I went back to my body and just felt relaxed and peaceful. And the feelings I'd had of jealousy or competitiveness just went away.

As a result of her OBE, this eight-year-old child had amazing insight and understanding. All of our OBEs have great value as a window onto insight. They give us an enlightened perspective, and allow us to laugh at the things we sometimes take so seriously, so unhappily. OBEs also affirm that there is indeed an afterlife, and that we do not give up anything at all when our bodies die.

Do you recall OBEs from your childhood? If you think back, you may remember them as unusual happenings, strange ideas or childhood fantasies. But if you look closer, you will understand that your childhood OBEs were very real events that have been discounted or forgotten.

Magic and Repressed OBEs

Why have we forgotten our childhood OBEs? Socially unacceptable, threatening or fearful events are sometimes repressed, so that we have no conscious memory of them. Children love their parents dearly, and will often do anything to please them, including giving up the very joyful practice and memory of OBE. Fortunately, we can let go of fear and remember unconscious repressed OBEs from childhood. Remembering a forgotten OBE is like finding a lost ring given to you by someone you love very deeply.

Sometimes we are afraid of what we believe to be intangible or magical experiences. Recently, a scientist confessed to us that he was afraid of electricity, because turning on a light seemed like magic to him. What magical or inexplicable things are you afraid of? There are obviously a tremendous number of things going on in our world that are beyond our raw physical senses.

Consider the spectrum of light. The optical slice of light that we see with our eyes is a very small part of the full spectrum. Yet we tend to think that only what we can see with our own eyes is real. What we see is a translation of the reality. Different people see the same light differently. Air is another good example. We cannot see air, so we assume there is not much to it. Yet it holds multi-ton aircraft aloft and keeps our bodies alive with every breath we take.

When we are very calm and quiet, we can often understand magic and perceive things which are lost in the background noise of modern life. We can recover forgotten or repressed experiences when we allow ourselves to become very quiet. And when we begin to accept the unacceptable, miracles happen.

As children, all of us enjoyed the miracle of OBEs. And most of us adults continue to have OBEs, but we typically forget, repress or discount them because of fear of social recrimination. When we try to communicate the inexpressible beauty of an OBE to someone who is not understanding, it can be a painful and very lonely experience. Fortunately there are many, many people with whom we can share our OBEs, because they have been there. In fact, not only can we talk about our OBEs, we can literally experience the same, simultaneous OBE if we have a special connection with someone. Can you imagine how wonderful it feels to share, completely and perfectly, the kaleidoscope of expanded awareness and deepest feelings with someone you love?

Some of our dreams are actually OBEs, but are often discounted as no more than vivid dreams. OBE "dreams" are different in that they have special characteristics of awareness and control. This lucidity may include a view of the dreamer's body asleep in bed. It is easy to distinguish an OBE from a dream. An OBE has no unreal or illogical elements and is often quite mundane. Of course, dreams can contain apparent nonsense. An OBE is extremely vivid and lucid, whereas a dream may be murky and full of non-sequiturs. Finally, an OBE is always beautiful and positive. If you had a negative experience, then it was probably a dream.

Do you dream of flying? Flying dreams are often OBEs. And they are highly cherished OBEs, because they are very sensual and create lingering feelings of exhilaration. Perhaps this is why many practitioners refer to their OBEs simply as "flying," when discussing them with accepting individuals.

Anesthesia and Near-death OBEs

Many surgeons and nurses have heard their patients recount operating room events which occurred while the patients were deeply anesthetized, or even clinically dead and subsequently revived. Individuals who experience this type of physically-induced OBE often report leaving their body, traveling through a long tunnel toward a beautiful light, visiting a world of beauty and meeting deceased relatives who instruct them to return to their bodies. There are literally thousands of documented cases of these near-death OBEs.

The following vignette is a verbatim transcription of a woman's fourth birthing experience. It is not a moment-of-death experience, but seems to be anesthesia related.

> *The birth of my child was a traumatic experience and I find myself reluctant to talk about it. I was in labor for such a long time, 35 or 36 hours. They were giving me pain killers — injections. The doctor came in and said that they had given me enough morphine for a 250 pound man, and they couldn't give me any more. So he was going to take me down to the delivery room and let the nurse just give me a little bit of gas every now and then to make me more comfortable. He said it was going to be a long time and it had already been forever — a day and a half. He suggested to my husband that he go get something to eat and come back later.*
>
> *They took me to the delivery room and did not strap me down. I was hurting very badly. I remember thinking that I wanted to breathe the gas really bad. The nurse put the mask up there and I jumped into it. At that moment, the first sensation I had was that I was dying. I thought I was suffocating and couldn't breathe, so I started fighting it. She did not have me strapped down when I started fighting it. Then she was screaming for people to help hold me down,*

and some people came running and they held me down and knocked me out.

I remember being above and watching myself hitting this woman, trying to get away from the gas, because I felt like I was suffocating. I remember watching this scene in the delivery room which to me looked identical to an operating room. I was watching this nurse yelling, watching myself hit her, being amazed at this incredible strength I had.

After my body was still, I saw the doctor run into the room and he was holding his hands up in the air and they were wet. He didn't have on rubber gloves. The nurse was screaming "The baby's coming; the baby's coming." The doctor delivered the baby without rubber gloves on. I remember thinking that the way they were positioning me on the table — if the doctor were not there, the baby would have fallen on the floor head first.

I was watching all this from above in a rather curious kind of way, watching these people panic and run around. I had some awareness that they were concerned about the fact that they hadn't anticipated the baby coming and that they were totally unprepared. It was a difficult experience on my body afterwards. The way they handled it was pretty traumatic.

When the doctor came in to see me the next day, I asked him about these images that I had and about the fact that I hit the nurse. I told him that I saw him running into the room and there were other people running. I described how he was holding his hands up and they were wet and he didn't have on rubber gloves. I asked him about all those experiences and he acted very uncomfortable, but quickly regained his composure, then denied them. He said that I had simply had a bad dream. Sometimes these bad dreams were common, when you were "put to sleep," he said.

So he dismissed my OBE and I accepted his explanation and thought surely that it didn't happen. Part of me always questioned it and wondered, but another part of me found it easy to accept the explanations of the God-like doctor.

Note that this womans's OBE was immediately discounted by the physician, probably because of his own fears. Then the patient discredited her own experience and accepted the doctor's explanation. It seems likely that this process of discreditation occurs frequently in medical environments. But did you know that there are support groups all over the world for those who have had near-death OBEs?

Ether, nitrous oxide, sodium pentothal and some other types of anesthesia appear to be strong inducements for OBE. However, these artificially-induced OBEs are generally less controllable and less lucid than naturally-occurring OBEs. Nevertheless, they often provide amazing insight.

There is an interesting paradox related to OBE and death. We have all heard stories of ghosts, witches, devils and haunted houses. Some people are afraid of OBE, because they mistakenly associate OBE with death. But in a very practical way, OBE affirms that there is an afterlife, and that we do not give up anything at all when our bodies die. Just as talking about orgasm is completely different from experiencing orgasm, reading about spirituality is incomparable to experiencing yourself as spirit.

OBEs Motivated by Necessity

OBE is often done of necessity or convenience, and may not be considered at all remarkable by its user. For example, a guitarist who plays in a standing position cannot see his finger positions on the frets, because the guitar neck hangs at an awkward viewing angle. Some guitarists find that their technique improves if they see their guitar from the viewpoint of the audience. In other words, they look at themselves from outside of their body, so they do not have to rely on feel alone to orient their fingers. Guitarists, who have this OBE ability, report that what they see is not a mirror or reverse image. In fact, they find it confusing to stand in front of a mirror while playing. But if you ask these guitarists if they can do OBE, they will probably answer "no." What they do is to them simply a necessary and instinctual part of good guitar playing.

Here is a dramatic example of an OBE born of necessity. A man who was separated from his wife was prohibited from visiting her. His wife had just given birth and was resting in the hospital when he telephoned. She said that her father had hired security guards and would not allow him to see the baby. The husband began crying hysterically. Later when he calmed down, he suddenly left his body and went directly to his wife's hospital room. He watched the nurse come and change the baby's diaper and heard conversations between his wife and the nurse. He was able to describe everything in vivid detail, including conversations and events which occurred over an extended period of time. When he called his wife the next day to tell her about his amazing experience, she expressed disbelief saying that he must have passed by the security guards and been in her room. Yet he was more than 1500 miles away at the time.

Multi-faceted OBEs

This next account of OBE is especially interesting, because of its many facets. Note that this woman's OBE seemed to provide a type of protection against the physical pain and trauma of an accident. Also note that the woman predicted an event without a conscious reason for doing so. In addition, she was able to see past, present and future simultaneously.

> *It was a near-death experience, although not near death like some people talk about in surgery when their heart stops. It was a car wreck. We were on a long highway driving at dusk. The sun was setting and it was out in the desert*

somewhere between Phoenix and Las Vegas. I was in the passenger seat. The man I was with was driving fairly fast. I remember looking out the window, looking out toward the sky and desert. All of a sudden, I had this awareness that I was going to die.

I knew that the car was going to wreck and I had an awareness that I was going to die. It was like I went into some kind of trance and started out of my body prior to the moment the car wreck actually occurred. There was no fear, interestingly enough. There was not a tremendous fear of death, but a sort of resignation, an acceptance. Neither did I have a feeling of intense pleasure at that point. There was some worry, a moment of nagging concern that I was going to die, but not fear. I remember thinking that the only sad thing about it was that I would not get to experience my children, who were very young, as young women. I wanted to know them as young women and needed to see them grow up.

All this was so fascinating, because it happened in a flash. It could not have been more than five seconds, maybe ten seconds at the most. It wasn't fear and it wasn't — it was like past, present, and future. I could see it all. It was like everything was frozen, but not only was it frozen; also, I could see past, present and future. I could see it all and it was all the same and it was all right then and there happening at once.

It is totally indescribable. I'm not doing a very good job of describing it, but it was almost like the frozen frame of a movie, a picture that contained the beginning of the picture, the middle of the picture and the end of the picture. And I remember my last thought was, "Well, wait a minute — this is not an appropriate time. This can't be happening, because my children are very young and I want to see them grow into young women." Then there was sadness, an awareness of deep sadness about not being with my children as young women. It was like I willed something to change at that point.

Immediately, I experienced the car going through the desert and the sand coming in the windows and all the myriad of stuff flying around in the car and watching the car, watching the desert sand as the car went tumbling through the desert. Numerous things were hitting my body and my body was thrashing around in the car against the dashboard and things in the car were flying around and things outside flying into the car. My head was banging around the dashboard and the windshield.

Strangely, I was feeling no pain, no pain whatsoever. All this seemed to happen in slow motion and yet, in a split second. As I watched this happening to myself, the most fascinating thing about it was the awareness that it was happening before it actually happened. When everything stopped still (The car stopped; the sand stopped; everything stopped.), then I was pulled back into my body. Then there was just this eerie silence, complete silence. I knew I was alive, and I also knew I was OK instantly, but the silence was eerie.

Note that this woman's attitude toward impending death was free from fear. She had an automatic acceptance of her death until she focused on her children. Then she was able to affirm the importance of her children and her strong desire to know them as young adults. Moreover, this woman apparently felt a sense of free choice and willed herself to live. Certainly, this experience provided multiple levels of insight for this individual.

Reports of insight-oriented OBEs seem to be more frequent among gurus, rabbis, saints, priests, ministers, and others revered as "holy" people. Why would these groups have more insight-oriented OBEs? Many religious systems require rigorous discipline in meditation, prayer, diet and daily routine. And some religious groups have elaborate rituals designed to produce a mystical union with God. Perhaps these lifestyles are more conducive to OBE. Or it may be that these individuals remember more OBEs, because it is more acceptable to report them if one is a "holy" person.

We can all enjoy the benefits of insight-oriented OBEs. It really can be very easy and we certainly don't have to wait for some traumatic event. Simply by practicing the exercises in this book, we can expand our awareness and develop new, dynamic insights. For all of us who have searched for spiritual answers and questioned the meaning of life, OBEs will provide answers. It is much more potent and illuminating to experience ourselves as spiritual beings than to just read about religion. And once we have shared the ecstasy of spiritual bonding, we have wonderful insights about ourselves and our relationships.

Environmentally Induced OBEs

There is an occupation that, by its very nature, tends to induce a particular type of OBE. We have known several deep sea divers, not scuba divers, but oil-field divers. These guys are the John Waynes of the ocean oil fields. One of the things they do is lay pipe from the rigs to the shore, using huge equipment in very dark, dangerous conditions.

When these divers are doing depth dives, they live in compression chambers which are built like oval cylinders about 30 feet long and eight feet in diameter. There are bunk beds along each wall, a shower, sink, commode and a storage area for equipment. Six men with all their equipment live in this small area for approximately 30 days at a time. While in the compression chamber, the divers breathe a mixture of helium and oxygen.

Since there is essentially no walking or sitting area, the divers are either lying in their bunks or working below. A diving bell attaches to the side of the chamber. Two men go down in the bell, one man goes out and works and the other stays in the bell to monitor gases and maintain communication. They work four-hour shifts, twenty-four hours per day.

Once in the compression chamber, the divers are essentially trapped and cannot easily leave. It may take two or three days to decompress. So if a man is injured, they can send a doctor in, but they cannot get the injured man out quickly. Of course, if they decide to send a doctor in, then they have seven people in that very small space.

These divers are subjected to a tremendous amount of sensory deprivation. The average person cannot adapt to this degree of sensory deprivation without negative consequences. Divers often complain of an ever-increasing longing for women, fresh air, blue skies, "the beach," the color green, alcohol, exercise, cigarettes, family, friends and "a normal life."

It is interesting to note that these divers often speak of the compression chamber as the "womb" and refer to their life-support hoses as their umbilical cords. Indeed, the womb metaphor seems rather appropriate. In their "womb," they are fed and nurtured and supplied with breath by the mother ship. They have lost freedom and have little control over what happens to them.

In order to give up their freedom and cope with the severe deprivation, the divers apparently enter altered states of consciousness for significant periods of time. Thus, they are able to let days drift by, and after a while time ceases to have meaning for them. They are aware of time only in relation to money and report that "The cash register rings every day." However, they often do not know if it is morning or night and their days may tend to run together.

A consistent type of OBE is reported by the divers. They refer to it as their "Cinderella dreams." These "dreams" are very vivid experiences of leaving the chamber, going to the beach, seeing the sand, grass and trees, watching people (especially women), and just "playing." There was so much commonality in their dream reports that we became fascinated with them. Gradually, it became apparent that they were having OBEs.

During these dreams, they all reported an awareness of a necessity to be back in the chamber within a certain amount of time: "I knew that I could go to the beach and play, but I'd have to be back by a certain time." It was reported that they instinctively knew when to return. This belief about returning by a non-specified deadline led them to label their experiences "Cinderella dreams."

It appears that common environmental factors of severe sensory deprivation, abnormal blood gases (helium and oxygen mixture), high motivation and ASCs are responsible for the consistency among the deep sea divers' OBEs. Note that the divers' OBEs are artificially-induced OBEs, even though they are motivated by pleasure.

Of course, naturally-occurring OBEs are often motivated by pleasure, too. A friend told us of a technique that she taught herself, which has immensely increased her pleasure of SAWNKI. She describes herself as an avid voyeur. So she decided to "mentally" stand beside the bed and watch herself and her husband having sex. This variation has created nights of great ecstasy for her. Although she cannot always observe herself in this way, she has learned to increase the frequency of her successes. She describes her "viewing" from the visual perspective of one standing at the foot of the bed, yet has no idea that she is having a true OBE.

Characteristics of OBEs

Naturally-occurring out-of-body experiences are very joyful, normal human activities which are widespread among the general public. They evoke a sense of being intimately in touch with all creation and are characterized by feelings of exhilaration, freedom and peace. These pleasurable feelings linger for days. OBEs make us high and are very beneficial to our mental and physical health. We have generally found OBE practitioners to be happy and well-adjusted.

OBEs demonstrate the existence of the mind separate from the brain and the body. They tend to increase our beliefs in personal immortality and remove our fears of death. Of course, OBEs also provide new, dynamic insights of great value. But most importantly, OBEs are very gratifying experiences which allow us to embrace the ecstasy we all seek, an ecstasy we have felt before and will feel again.

All OBEs include a projection or extension of awareness beyond the physical location of the body and a knowledge that the experience is very, very real. But there are many variations among OBEs. We have described OBEs where the body is immobile, and others where the body is active. There is not a single, unique set of traits which defines a "true" OBE.

Sometimes, visual acuity during OBE allows reading of printed words in the dark, but sometimes words are indistinct. Some people have OBEs with their eyes closed and some with their eyes open. While out of their body, most people do not hear spoken words, but rather sense exact thoughts and emotions. It is the same way with reading. While out of the body, we know what the ideas are within the words, but we may not necessarily see the literal words, especially if they are written in a foreign language.

The stages and characteristics of OBE vary among individuals. The onset of an OBE may be signaled by a floating or a sinking sensation. Or an OBE may begin with a rather intense vibration of the whole body. Buzzing, ringing or roaring sounds may precede an OBE. Some people travel during an OBE by flying over the ground, while some leap instantly from one location to the next. Some individuals see a silver cord or an apparitional figure and some simply don't care about those things. After returning to the body, some people have an illusion of paralysis (catalepsy), although they are resting in a very natural way. These individuals are reassured to know that they can begin to awaken their body by simply moving a finger slightly.

Just as there are no two identical people, there are no two identical OBEs. There is little to be gained by worrying whether or not one is doing OBE "correctly." There is much to be gained by simply relaxing into the experience without attempting to categorize it.

A Fun Recall of Childhood OBEs

Here is a fun exercise that will allow you to recall some of your early childhood OBEs. We have all been out of our bodies as children, but may have simply forgotten our experiences. It is like remembering a dream. Sometimes we may think that we spent a restful night without dreaming, because we do not remember our dreams of that night. Yet we all dream every night and we all have OBEs.

You may read the exercise a couple of times and then simply lie down, relax and experience it. Or you may prefer to listen to a tape recording of the exercise. By the way, if you have never had a professional, hour-long massage, now is a good time to treat yourself by hiring a masseuse. Then you will truly know what it feels like to be completely relaxed.

> Begin the process of relaxing. Take a couple of deep breaths, breathing deeply, exhaling slowly and completely. Allow your body total freedom, relaxing deeply and completely.
>
> Now begin with your toes and feel the waves of relaxation spreading from your toes up into your legs, soothing waves of relaxation, stroking. Relaxation is continuing to spread up your legs into your thighs, into your hips

and the pelvic region of your body. Feel the beautiful waves of relaxation — wave after wave of gentle, refreshing relaxation spreading throughout your pelvic region, your stomach and your back. Enjoy these repetitive, stroking, soothing waves of relaxation as they spread up your back and deep inside your body. Feel the ripples of relaxation spreading throughout your back, your stomach, your chest — caressing and soothing, up your body and down your arms to the tingling tips of your fingers. Repetitive waves of relaxation are rhythmically stroking and caressing all the way up to the very top of your head. You are so relaxed — freely, deeply, wonderfully relaxed.

Now that you are relaxed, begin to experience a return to the wonderment of your special laughing place, a laughing place of childhood. When you were a child, there was a special place deep inside of you — a laughing place — that you enjoyed again and again.

Take a moment to return to that special laughing place of childhood. Let yourself visualize colors. As you focus on flowing colors, recall the little child, or perhaps an older child. Feel the special laughing within, the fun activities. Perhaps you will recall going to school, playing baseball, swinging high in a swingset or splashing in the water. And there were those times — when you, in your quiet moments, quiet moments inside of yourself — took special journeys outside of your body. Some might say those were fantasies, but you understand these special journeys of pleasure. As a child, you gave yourself permission to leave your body easily and automatically. Your skills in flying free were so very good — spontaneous, easy.

Now continue to remember; enjoy the memory of the small child within — emerging and floating free, returning to the magic sugarland of childhood. Everything was new and fresh, magical and easy. Experience drifting and floating. See the little child — that little child who is still there within you. As you embrace the little child within, you'll remember an out of body experience, an experience of free flight for fun or perhaps because of boredom. Recall a wonderful free flight out of your body. It may have occurred because of high motivation, something you wanted to see or experience.

Allow yourself the complete joy of experiencing — the playful fun, the joy of flying free out of your body — seeing, feeling, and knowing in a very special way. You are flying free in a very pleasurable, knowing, laughing way. Feel rainbows and breezes, moonbeams and clouds, while you are flying free out of your body. You are flying free like a bird, a butterfly or a leaf in the wind. Gently savor and enjoy the recall of your free flights of childhood; flying into rainbows and sunlight, flying above other children, drifting like a balloon in the wind, or floating like a translucent, iridescent soap bubble — floating gently out of your body.

Perhaps you will enjoy recalling a particular out-of-body experience of childhood. Or, you may remember bits and pieces of several flights of joy. As you recall these experiences of fun, joy and wonderment, you understand how very easy and natural, how very spontaneous and automatic, it was to leave your body. A part of you always knew, as you watched the birds, butterflies, drifting balloons and the leaves in the wind. Recall the wind — the wind, which is felt and experienced and enjoyed. The wind cannot be seen, but you know it is there. You are the wind, free, flying free . . . drifting. As a little child, you knew how easy it was to fly — like a bird, a butterfly, a balloon or a leaf in the wind.

As a child, you knew how to turn cartwheels above the children and teacher in school. You could float above the trees, leave your body and float out the window of your room. You could fly outside and play in the rain or do any of a thousand other things. As a child, it happened all the time, flying free. You may experience again this free flight out of your body just like a little child.

Now that you have enjoyed a playful journey back into childhood, you may remember more and more. Your awareness blossoms as you go about your daily life, enjoying the routine, simple things and the complex challenges of your life. From time to time, special vivid memories of free flights from childhood may be beautifully recalled. It will be like remembering a special playmate that you had forgotten. This will occur spontaneously and naturally. There is nothing that you need do. The seed has been planted and watered, nurtured and warmed. So it automatically brings forth beautiful flowers — joyful memories of those childhood free flights. Let all your recollections be wonderful, expansive memories of joy that automatically promote health, tranquility, peace and harmony throughout your mind and body.

When you are ready to return to the present moment, you will naturally begin the process of awakening. Let yourself wake up slowly, gently. Become aware of the wonderful, restful, refreshed feeling in your body. Let yourself count out loud, counting from one to ten, waking up more and more with each count. Simply by counting, you will feel wonderfully alert and energized.

Affirmations

Are you now observing alterations of consciousness in yourself and others more frequently? Do you find it easier to shift your awareness whenever you wish? As you continue to recall your naturally-occurring OBEs, you will automatically affirm your spiritual/sexual self and know that you are making significant progress toward a goal of ecstasy and limitless intimacy.

Copy and post the affirmations you like best in a prominent place. Or, you may simply wish to read them from the book each evening before retiring. It is perfectly natural to like some affirmations more than others. Feel free to modify them in whatever way pleases you.

1. I am more than body and brain — I am eternal, everlasting spirit.

2. My mind is free and the positive expansion of my consciousness is limitless.

3. I freely and automatically shift my awareness to maximize my pleasure.

4. I rejoice with the understanding that I can get high naturally and fly free easily.

5. I embrace this new opportunity for the glorious expression of all my gifts.

6. I am a beautiful creation of the divine union of sex and spirit.

7. I eagerly anticipate crossing my natural bridges to ecstasy.

8. I am blessed with the increasing memory of my natural childhood OBEs.

9. I nurture the child within and express my vibrant sexual energy.

10. I recognize my spiritual self and cherish my personal sexual evolution.

Selected Readings

Bach, Richard. *The Bridge Across Forever*, Dell Publishing, New York, 1984.

Blackmore, Susan. "Out-of-body Experiences in Schizophrenia: a Questionnaire Survey," *Journal of Nervous and Mental Disease*, Oct 1986, vol 174(10), pp615-619.

Crookall, Robert. *The Study and Practice of Astral Projection*, Aquarian Press, London, 1961.

Crookall, Robert. *Casebook of Astral Projection*, University Books, Secaucus, New Jersey, 1972.

Dossey, Larry. *Recovering the Soul: A Scientific and Spiritual Search*, Bantam Books, New York, 1989.

Friends of IANDS, (support group for people who have had Near Death Experiences), Dept. of Psychiatry, University of Connecticut Health Center, Farmington, Connecticut.

Green, Celia. *Out-of-The-Body Experiences,* Institute of Psychophysical Research, Oxford, England, 1968.

Jones, Gabbert, and Twemlow. "Psychological and Demographic Characteristics of Persons Reporting Out-of-body Experiences," *Hillside Journal of Clinical Psychiatry*, 1984, vol 6(1), pp105-115.

Kubler-Ross, Elisabeth. *On Death and Dying*, MacMillan Publishing Co., Inc., New York, 1969.

Mitchell, Janet Lee. *Out-of-Body Experiences: A Handbook*, Ballantine Books, New York, 1981.

Monroe, Robert A. *Journeys Out of the Body*, Anchor Books, Garden City, New York, 1977.

Moody, Jr., Raymond. *Life After Life*, Bantam Books, New York, 1975.

Moody, Jr., Raymond. *The Light Beyond*, Bantam Books, New York, 1988.

Muldoon, Sylvan. *The Case for Astral Projection*, Aries Press, Chicago, 1946.

Palmer, John, and Vasser, C. " ESP and Out-of-Body Experiences: An Exploratory Study," *Journal of the American Society for Psychical Research*, 1974, vol 68, pp257-280.

Ring, Kenneth. *Heading Toward Omega: In Search of the Meaning of the Near-death Experience*, Quill Publishing, New York, 1984.

Rogo, Scott. "Researching the Out-of-body Experience: The State of the Art," *Anabiosis*, Spring 1984, vol 4(1), pp21-49.

Rogo, Scott. *Leaving the Body: A Complete Guide to Astral Projection*, Prentice Hall Press, New York, 1983.

Sheldrake, Rupert. *A New Science of Life*, St. Martin's Press, New York, 1983.

Stack, Richard. *Out-of-Body Adventures: 30 Days to the Most Exciting Experience of Your Life,* Contemporary Books, New York, 1988.

Tobacyk and Mitchell. "The Out-of-body Experience and Personality Adjustment," *Journal of Nervous and Mental Disease,* June 1987, vol 175(6), pp367-370.

3

RELAXING INTO PEACEFUL EXPECTATIONS

A Tantalizing Invitation

As glorious spiritual entities we are blessed with the gift of ever-expanding awareness. We can freely and easily shift our awareness to maximize our pleasure. Our free-flowing minds provide us with abundant opportunities for the creation of ecstasy and limitless intimacy. When we allow our bodies to become deeply relaxed, we can automatically direct our minds into sensuous altered states of consciousness. ASCs induced with relaxation open the door and invite spontaneous out-of-body experiences.

When we invite guests into our home, we want to help them feel relaxed and comfortable. We welcome invited guests, but never demand that anyone come into our home. It is the same way with OBE. We cannot force an OBE; we cannot demand that it happen. If we try too hard, we often end up frustrated. The opposite of trying too hard is relaxing into peaceful expectations.

If we think to ourselves, "I'd like to have an OBE, but I know I can't," then the harder we try, the less successful we become.

Perhaps it is less a matter of achieving OBE and more a process of allowing ourselves to relax into the joy of OBE. Likewise, the best sex happens when we let go of the need for achievement and become lost in the joy of sex. A classic example of trying too hard is the man who ejaculates prematurely. Instead of relaxing and enjoying sex, he is trying very hard to delay orgasm. And the harder he tries to delay, the quicker he climaxes. So let's remember that trying too hard is usually self-defeating, especially when combined with negative thinking.

Have you ever wanted to seduce someone special? Did you try to make it happen? Of course we cannot make our dream lover respond, but we can offer a very tantalizing invitation. Relaxation is a very tantalizing invitation for OBE — a delicious, irresistible invitation.

An OBE Invited by Relaxing

The following vignette is an example of a spontaneous OBE that was invited by simply relaxing and clearing the mind. Note that this man had no previous recall of OBE and was totally surprised by the event.

> *It was strange the way it happened, so suddenly, so unexpectedly. I'd never even heard of an out-of-body experience much less had one. I remember sitting at my desk at work. It had been a long day, a long week. I became aware of the aching tension in my neck and shoulders. Suddenly I had this feeling that I had to get away. I had to relax. I just couldn't take any more of the hassles that day. So I made up an excuse and left work early. And I don't know why, but I didn't go home. I found myself driving straight to the lake.*
>
> *It was one of those early, beautiful spring days when it feels so good to be outside, warm but pleasantly cool. And I took an old blanket that I kept in the trunk for working on the car and spread it out by the lake. But instead of lying down on*

the blanket, I began to walk, just walking beside the lake and trying to put all the hassles of work out of my mind. I couldn't seem to let go of the worry and anger and frustration that I felt. I couldn't seem to stop thinking about it and the tension wouldn't leave. I found myself becoming angrier because the tension wouldn't leave. So I started running furiously, as though to run away from the ever-present, worrying thoughts in my head. I ran and ran and ran, until I couldn't run anymore.

Then I was conscious only of breathing and my heart pounding in my chest. I walked slowly, gasping for breath, listening only to the sound of my labored breathing. I walked and walked like a robot. But gradually, I became aware of the sound of the water lapping gently against the shoreline and the birds singing. At last, my mind was clear — blank. And I became fascinated by the silver sparkles of light across the surface of the water.

As I walked down the small hill toward my old blanket, I was overwhelmed with the beauty of the place. Strange — I had never noticed it before in the same way. Three couples had positioned themselves on top of picnic tables. They were sprinkled some distance away from each other, some distance from my blanket. I had the feeling that each was seeking privacy, but more importantly, that no one wanted to intrude on the privacy of another.

I sat down on the blanket and stared at the lake. The sun was beginning a slow descent and the surface of the water was becoming ablaze with color. A gentle, cool breeze was creating tingling, cold chills across my sweaty skin. I remember thinking that this was as close to heaven as it gets. Then I was startled by the sound of an angel singing and looked to see a young woman on the top of the hill behind me. She was sitting under a tree, strumming a guitar and singing a ballad to no one in particular. I remember think-

ing that she had the sweetest voice that I've ever heard. I laughed at myself, my reflection on heaven.

I lay on my blanket and felt an indescribable kind of peace. Work and daily hassles seemed far away—a long, long way, away. Somehow the things which had upset me earlier in the day seemed ridiculous, silly. I was watching the leaves in the tree overhead, fluttering gently in the breeze. And then it happened! Suddenly I felt this sensation of floating, like I was floating in the air—floating like I'd never felt before, not like on a boat, or rubber raft or in a swimming pool. I can't describe it. Anyway, I was floating and then I was standing in front of the girl who was singing on top of the hill. I was fascinated by her fingers moving on the strings of the guitar. I felt blessed by the sweetness of her voice. I don't recall the words. The words made no difference. The blissful message of love was clear.

I don't know how much time passed, but at some point I looked down the hill and saw myself lying on the blanket. I thought, "Oh, no, this can't be happening because I'm lying on the blanket at the bottom of the hill." I felt a sense of panic and thought "Maybe I'm dead." Immediately, I felt my whole body vibrating and heard a strange ringing in my ears. Then there was a brief feeling of immobility, before I again became aware that I was watching the leaves fluttering in the breeze.

It was almost dark, but none of the couples had left. I wanted to hug my wife and children. I walked slowly to the car smiling to myself. As I walked past one of the couples, the young man looked at me and said simply, "It doesn't get any better than this." I smiled, but didn't reply. No reply was necessary. We all knew. When you have shared a bit of heaven, you know.

We can all embrace a little bit of heaven. It occurs when we believe in heaven, when we relax and place ourselves in a position to receive heaven. If we are still and quiet, we can see the beauty and feel the ecstasy. Sometimes it is important to ask the right question, too. For example, we could ask ourselves, "Can I really do OBE?" Or we could ask, "When will I experience myself out of my body again?" An attitude of belief and expectation arises naturally when we realize that OBE is just another common altered state of consciousness.

Stress and Tension

Have you been relaxed today? Or have you felt tension in your neck, shoulders and back? Have you rushed through your day with a sense of time urgency, feeling overwhelmed with too many things to do? Does your mind often become cluttered with worry, anxiety or negative thoughts? Do you have trouble unwinding at the end of your day? If you answered yes to any of these questions, you are not alone.

As human beings we are subjected to immense amounts of stress. Rapidly changing social roles, job insecurities, time pressures, negative emotions, technical advancements, ambiguous situations and negative thinking are just a few of the stress-inducing factors that we face on a daily basis. It seems that with each generation, additional stress is added to our lives. Is it any wonder that we tend to look longingly backward to simpler, more peaceful times? Fortunately, there is a way to become more peaceful and relaxed. And the best news is that it can be very easy.

Healthy babies and young children have an innate ability for complete muscle relaxation. Observe a young child at play and notice how loose and flexible he is. Pick up a sleeping child and feel how limp her muscles are. With practice, we can all become as children again, relaxing naturally and completely.

When we were infants, we had a natural talent for deep muscle relaxation. But we were also born with an ability to evoke a defensive reaction called the "fight or flight" response. This response is easily observed in animals. For example, a frightened cat will momentarily freeze, tensing muscles, arching its back and forcing its hair to stand on end. Like the cat, we instinctively, unconsciously evoke the "fight or flight" response. But unlike the cat, we make the response too often, reacting again and again to frequent changes and daily stressors. And unlike the cat, we can neither run nor fight in most situations.

Our complex urban society has encouraged us to make the "fight or flight" response too frequently. What this means for most of us is that we are walking around with trapped muscular tension. It is as though our nerve cells are standing at attention like the hair on the cat's back. And even when we think we are relaxing, we often have significant residual tension.

The Relaxation Response

There are many sensuous and pleasurable ways to smooth away our residual tension and invite OBE. While you have been enjoying the exercises in this book, you have also increased your skill in making the relaxation response. The relaxation response can easily be created by structured exercises such as tensing and relaxing muscles, fantasizing and visualizing, or focusing on positive sensory stimuli. It can also be created by positive activities like sex, laughter, hugging, taking warm showers or physical exercise. Can you think of other delectable ways to relax?

The relaxation response is not simply sleep or rest. Actually, some of us are quite tense while we rest and may grind our teeth, clench our fists or worry obsessively when we sleep. The relaxation response is a "letting go" of tension until the muscles become completely loose and limp, and the nervous system becomes still. It is a calming of the body and a quieting of the mind, until the mind becomes blank and peaceful. The deepest relaxation creates ASCs which are ecstatic, beautiful windows that increase our vision and allow our spirits to fly free.

Throughout history, techniques for creating the relaxation response have existed as part of our cultural and religious teachings. We have discovered several easy steps to relaxation. When we relax, we begin by creating a pleasurable, supportive environment. Then we loosen our clothing, position our bodies comfortably and let our muscles become limp. We embrace a passive attitude by clearing or focusing our minds. And then we develop a beautiful, enchanting emotional state and simply enjoy. Yoga, prayer, and meditation are examples of techniques which help us create relaxation and promote inner peace, tranquility and spiritual harmony.

Relaxing into an experience and letting it unfold naturally is really a matter of allowing ourselves to be quiet. For example, get away from the city lights and lie under the stars. Rather than picking out one constellation from the next, and naming them all, just allow your consciousness to expand into the heavens. Feel the feelings, but avoid naming them. You will soon discover that you have invited an ethereal state of relaxation.

A Love Exercise

In order to feel relaxed and peaceful, and to become part of a deeper contentment, it is helpful to allow ourselves to be filled with love, to understand how very lovable we are, to know that we are loved and to feel it deep inside of ourselves. The next exercise is designed to evoke that deep feeling of complete and fulfilling love. Then relaxation and peace occur automatically. Worries drift away and things which once bothered us become trivial and unimportant.

Perhaps in the past you have thought, "I wish my lover would say, 'I love you' more often." Or perhaps you have lamented, "I just don't feel loved; I know that I am loved, but I don't feel lovable." This exercise allows you to experience and to feel love, and to know you are feeling it. You may do it alone or with a partner. If you do it alone, you will need a large mirror that you can position in front of you, so that you can sit comfortably in front of the mirror and relax. If you decide to do it with a partner, you will need to choose positions that allow you to look into each others' eyes comfortably.

Begin by clearing your space, the physical space around you and the private space within. If you wish, you may use candles, incense or soft music in the distance. It may be helpful to play a recorded tape of the exercise.

Simply sit down and focus your attention on the eyes. Forget everything that you ever knew about love. Forget everything you ever knew about this person. Just look into those beautiful, wonderful, reflective eyes.

> Begin to breathe deeply, slowly, rhythmically — relaxing more and more with each soft, easy, free and gentle breath you take. As you are breathing slowly and gently, you become aware that you are breathing in the very essence of life. You share the very essence of other people, plants, animals, the universe. The very breath that you breathe is the sweet essence of life and love. The air you breathe is shared with your deepest love again and again.
>
> Slowly now you are becoming aware of your reflection in the eyes, images bouncing back and forth. You can see a halo of light beginning to form around your partner, a beautiful radiant light shimmering and twinkling. Take a moment to look within and find your own heart. Experience it filling with love. As you expand with each breath, the heart center within fills with love.
>
> Begin to repeat silently the word "love." Focus your eyes on the eyes in front of you, knowing that you are

sending light and love to your mirror image, and receiving light and love in turn. Continue to repeat the word "love" silently as you experience a halo all around you and your partner. Your tongue and lips may move softly, as you continue saying the word "love" over and over. It is so beautiful, so wonderful.

The energy of love expands to fill your entire body and the room around you, until finally there is so much love that your tongue and lips cease to move. Your mind continues to repeat the word "love" at an ever-increasing rate, thousands of times faster than your mouth could ever form the sounds, so very fast. And the mind hears thousands of times faster than the ear. You are transmitting and receiving love in great abundance. And the more love you transmit, the more you receive.

You are now filled with all the love of the universe. You now have all the love that you have always wanted. Still your mind continues to repeat "love" and you are experiencing the vibrations, the light and the energy of love. You continue repeating it, breathing the air that is shared by all, until you become love — until it is impossible to separate yourself from the essence of love. And the love that you have always wanted, is there — perfect, pure, abundant love.

Just relax and allow the experience to take you as far as you wish to go. You may move your awareness to maximize your pleasure. Or you may merge together, becoming one reflecting pool of love. All the delicious choices are yours to enjoy.

The distance has gone away. When this much love is within you and all around you, you are profoundly relaxed. Everything else is trivial and unimportant. You have become the essence of life. Your shoulders are loose and limp, and your body is relaxed in every way.

As you go about your daily life, let this peaceful relaxation remain with you throughout every hour of every day.

Practice this love exercise once a day, for a week. Each time you may find that you are doing it for an extended period, yet it feels like minutes. You may wish to alternate the mirror and partner techniques. By the end of the week you will feel a new kind of contentment and inner peace that becomes a permanent part of you.

A Personal Relaxation Ritual

The love exercise is a viable model for creating your own personal relaxation ritual. It prohibits mind-wandering with the use of the "love" mantra and focuses awareness on positive emotions. The mantra is a word or phrase which eliminates worrying or distracting thoughts. It turns off your internal tape player, which is often analyzing and criticizing. Feel free to choose your own mantra and develop those techniques that feel right to you. The silent repetition of your own name may be very effective. We often choose words like "peace, quiet, calm, relax and deeper" as our mantras. In addition, we enjoy fixating on the sounds of the ocean, rain, wind and waterfalls.

You have already found how nice it is to relax in the earlier chapters. If you are not already relaxing on a regular basis, say fifteen minutes a day, now is a very good time to start. You may choose any method that works for you. Some of the techniques we recommend are hypnosis, biofeedback, yoga, meditation, exercise, prayer and sex. One key to these approaches is breathing; you want to arrive at a place where your breathing is slow, deep, rhythmic and completely unself-conscious. Your heart and mind will then become quiet.

You may want to enroll in a class in yoga, meditation or self-hypnosis. Practicing with a group is more powerful than individual practice for some of us. Or you may wish to simply practice the exercises in this book until you are satisfied with your skill level. If you are already skilled with one of these techniques, then you have a very good bridge to OBE. Remember that you are unique and special, so you will build your own personal bridges to OBE.

We are all unique and wonderful, and there is a special place each of us can go to find peace and harmony. It is a place inside of us. It is the same, and yet different for each of us. If you visualize it, you may see a steamy bend in a primordial jungle path, or you may see a formal garden, or you may simply see and hear a waterfall of light. There are as many facets to heaven as there are facets of humanity. When you relax in your special way each day, go to that special place where you can open yourself to the universe.

It is helpful to clear a private physical space to welcome OBE while you are clearing an emotional space. You could have a special room or chair or a tree beside a brook. You will develop a unique relaxation ritual that works for you. Perhaps you will have a special shirt or robe made of silk, velvet or satin that you will want to reserve just for relaxation. Maybe you will choose to lie nude on a soft fur rug or sit in front of a warm fireplace. You could take a sensuous bubble bath or enjoy a hot shower as part of your ritual. You may like to dim the lights or make the room very bright. You may wish to light candles, burn incense or fixate on a special picture. And there may be some special music or sounds that you find relaxing. The important thing is to choose pleasurable stimuli that help you relax. Just create a beautiful haven, a place where you can relax and fly free.

A Relaxed Lifestyle

To relax into peaceful expectations, it may be helpful to develop a more relaxed lifestyle. We have found it beneficial to avoid caffeine, drugs, alcohol, tobacco and non-natural substances. It also seems advantageous to eat healthily but lightly, since digestive processes may interfere with relaxation. Simple, moderate and pleasurable exercise is beneficial, because when we stretch muscles they automatically relax more completely. Let's remember that each choice is just a matter of discovering what works for us and then trusting our feelings.

There comes a time when we must simply let go and trust our feelings and ourselves. And it is helpful to realize that we have no beginning and no end. We have always been and always will be. So relax every day and trust your feelings, but don't try to schedule an OBE. Wait until it feels right; you'll know when. Sometimes an individual works for weeks trying to induce an OBE, then has the experience a day after giving up.

We have created mythical time urgencies which make us tense. Time has no reality. It is only a funny way of looking at things. If someone asks us what time it is, we could look at a clock, or we could simply answer "now." If someone asks us where we are, we could cheerfully answer "here." These answers help us let go of false, time urgencies and remind us to stay focused on the important facets of life.

How often do you use words like "must, should, ought to and have to?" We have observed that our spoken and mental language often contains many of these "urgency" words. To feel more relaxed and peaceful, we can avoid "urgency" words and substitute "freedom" words like "choose, desire, prefer and want to."

We have all heard about the benefits of positive thinking and speaking. So why do we catch ourselves saying negative words like "can't, won't, awful and terrible?" Perhaps it is because the myths of urgency and negativity continue in our society. But we can erase these myths. When we consistently have joyful expectations, we are rewarded with peace and ecstasy. Let's fill our awareness with free and positive, joyful and enthusiastic words and images. We will then become prisms reflecting exquisite rainbows of happiness.

One of the most wonderful paradoxes about OBE is that it usually occurs when we have a positive mental expectation and a sense of joy within — but, the experience of OBE dramatically increases our pleasure and positive emotions. It is like an ever-expanding sphere of joy.

We can invite OBE by encouraging positive thoughts and feelings, such as hope, faith, love, joy, peace and confidence. And laughter is a melody which welcomes OBE. If we seek humor and choose activities which make us laugh, we relax and become healthier, both physically and mentally . Hugs are another source of well-being. The more hugs we give and receive daily, the better we feel. Hug, smile and be happy. It is so easy, so simple, when we choose. One way or the other we always choose.

A Commune With Nature

Many poets and writers have described peace, tranquility and visions of ecstasy during their commune with nature. Names such as Wordsworth, Thoreau, Emerson and Longfellow come to mind. And how many spiritual leaders have spent forty days and forty nights in the wilderness and returned transformed? We have discovered — again and again — the magic of being outdoors in a beautiful place. Nature expands and transforms our perceptions of ourselves and our world. Myths of time urgency disappear and we feel free, relaxed and centered. Negativity vanishes, as we become entranced with beauty and wonderment.

Here is a delightful exercise that will help you commune with nature and relax into the present moment. With nature, you can learn how to expand your perceptions and truly experience wonderment. Walk in a park by yourself or with a close friend.

You may want to go barefoot, take off your underwear and wear as few clothes as practical. Consider the possibility that you have just awakened and found yourself in the Garden of Eden. Your eyes, ears and all of your senses are perceiving for the first time. And you are totally entranced with all the beauty around you.

Continue opening all of your senses more and more fully. As you walk, feel the air, see the colors and shapes, smell the leaves, listen to the birds and running water, touch the bark and soak up the sunlight. Enmesh yourself in feeling and perceiving. Forget about work, about home; forget about being on time. Become lost in the present moment and savor it sweetly. Just experience the totality of your surroundings, the timelessness of nature and the omnipresence of life. Perceive everything at once, allowing all of your senses to wash over you.

Watch an ant hill or a small eddy in a stream and imagine yourself to be living in that microcosmos. What does it feel like? Is their world any different from our world? Are we living in our own little worlds most of the time, too, oblivious to so much that is going on around us? OBE allows us to expand our little worlds into the cosmos which surrounds us.

When we are fully tuned in to our surroundings, when we realize that we are an inseparable part of everything around us, then we know that it makes no difference if the year is 1022 A.D. or 9000 B.C. It is almost as if people walking nearby cannot see us, except as an integral part of the landscape. We are not separate. We are not alone. The distance which we have felt is imaginary. We are a part of all living things and all living things are a part of us.

After completing the exercise, you can continue to share the joy by relaxing comfortably with your friend in a private place. Recall your walk in sensuous detail. Feel the images grow inside of you as you recall the experience. Go back and visit the park in your mind and paint a picture of it as you speak. Allow your awareness to move freely, expanding it until you feel yourself there in the park again. Express and savor the free and joyful feelings.

A Simple Miracle

When we really open ourselves to the possibilities of communion with nature, we are often blessed with miracles. The following vignette describes a simple OBE from a woman who has a special ability to relate with birds. The OBE occurred in the transition state between waking and dreaming. Although it was night and no lights were on, she could see clearly.

> *Some of my OBEs are so simple. I found myself in the garage. I was just looking around at everything from the perspective of being up near the ceiling. Most of the time when I have an OBE, I am up high somewhere looking down. That's the perspective that I tend to see things from. I went out into the garage and I was looking around. It occurred to me that I was looking for something, but I didn't know what. I was curious about what was out there.*
>
> *I wasn't aware of it previously, but a little bird had taken up residence in the garage. I confirmed this the next morning. Every night I close the garage door. So the next morning when I went into the garage, this little bird flew down and sat on the car just looking at me. He waited very patiently for me to open the garage door and then flew out.*
>
> *This continued for two or three weeks. At night he would be in the garage. And in the morning he would fly down to greet me. Strangely, he didn't seem to be afraid of me. It was as though we were friends. It seemed symbolic somehow. I wondered if he was showing me how easy it was to fly. I related it to my attempt to control OBEs. Like, all we need to do is open the door and then we can fly. We can allow*

ourselves to fly free and then return to the safety of our garages.

As a recent OBE practitioner, this woman had felt some unfounded fear and lack of self-confidence. Perhaps she was receiving the needed reassurance from this simple OBE. It is interesting to note that she had previously had wild birds fly to her and sit in her hand on several occasions. Apparently she had developed a special way of relating with birds.

> *When at home alone I sit,*
> *And am very tired of it,*
> *I have just to shut my eyes*
> *To go sailing through the skies—*
> *To go sailing far away*
> *To the pleasant Land of Play;*
> *To the fairy land afar*
> *Where the Little People are;*
>
> **Robert Louis Stevenson**

Reconnecting With the Child

Do you remember the first time you saw the play, Peter Pan, or the first time you saw the Wizard of Oz? Can you let the little child in you come out and play now? Do you remember the last time someone asked, "Will you play with me?" Weren't you happy when they asked?

Remember that OBE is fun; it is not work or study. Developing our childhood ability to play spontaneously and naturally is an easy and enjoyable path to OBE. If it isn't fun, then you took a wrong turn somewhere. Go back to that fork in the road and choose again. Go back to your childhood. Be a child. A truly mature person frequently invites the child within to play. Such a balanced, integrated person is not afraid to play even if others may think it inappropriate. The next time you find things around you getting too somber and serious, take a play break. Fly a paper airplane, watch cartoons, wade in a creek, dig in a sandbox, roll in the grass or ride a merry-go-round. Allow the child within you to emerge and play freely.

A simple way to reconnect with the child inside of you is to play with soap bubbles. Buy a jar of soap bubbles and carry it in your car. Then when you feel particularly tense during your day, stop in the nearest park and blow bubbles. Watch the floating, translucent bubbles and imagine that you are floating with them. Smile freely and let yourself be a child. Then get back in your car and carry the feeling with you. Remember that whatever our circumstances, we choose to feel the way we feel. We can choose to feel good.

We choose to play with our friends in a variety of ways. For example, we enjoy comedy shows and videos, cotton candy and popcorn, darts and shuffleboard. Also an hour or two splashing and relaxing together in a swimming pool or hot tub is always delightful for us. And there are a million other ways to play together. In any case, get in touch with the childlike wonderment within you by recalling and doing those things that you found especially delightful as a child. We have found it helpful to ask several friends to join us in making a list of things that were fun to do when we were children. What joy it is to share a different one each day for a week!

Children have more energy than adults because they give themselves permission to play. Here is an exercise that reminds us that we are abundant energy — more energy than matter, more spirit than body. Give a friend a firm massage for several minutes. Massage the legs, back, neck and shoulder muscles. Rub slowly and sensuously. Next give a light massage with the fingertips gliding over the skin. Take your time. Now, with your hands slightly cupped, very gently caress your partner's hair, moving down in repeated strokes from the crown to his shoulders. Do this slowly and lovingly, avoiding upward strokes. Let both people close their eyes and then begin to move your hands very slowly just above the skin of your friend. Feel the energy radiating between the two of you. These energy fields are always present, even though we may be unaware of them. Embracing the child inside of us and playing with others helps us to free our abundant energy and to bond with others in special ways.

OBE and Flying

Flying can help us understand OBE and relate to our spirituality. Soaring in a sailplane is an especially nice affirmation of our natural ability to fly. And learning to fly a sailplane can be a wonderful, healthful way to get high. Floating so silently on the air currents that we can surprise a bird from behind, we sense the real freedom within us. We become wind and sky, and accept that magic is as alive in the world as we are.

> *It's hard to be an agnostic up here in the Spirit of St. Louis, aware of the frailty of man's devices, a part of the universe between its earth and stars. If one dies, all this goes on existing in a plan so perfectly balanced, so wonderfully simple, so incredibly complex that it's far beyond our comprehension — worlds and moons revolving; planets orbiting on suns; suns flung with apparent recklessness through space. There's the infinite magnitude of the universe; there's the infinite detail of its matter — the outer star, the inner atom. And man conscious of it all —*
>
> **Charles A. Lindbergh**

Perhaps all you need to get started on the path to OBE is a single parasail ride. As you rise over the treetops, remember that so very much is just over the treetops of our awareness. All it takes is a little boost to see a farther horizon.

We tend to think of ourselves as solid, heavy, dense objects. We look at the numbers on the bathroom scale and think pounds of lead, pounds of lead. We see our shadow and think how solid we must be. But there is a simple way to show that we are really translucent. Hold a flashlight behind your hand in a darkened room. You will see the light pass right through your flesh. If you hold the flashlight against a nipple, the entire breast will glow. Place the lens of the light in your mouth, and your face will glow from within. Play with this for awhile and you will see that you are not as solid as you thought you were. Maybe you are a creature of light, after all.

Relaxing With Permission

By now you understand that attaining an altered state of consciousness is simple. OBE is just another ASC, accessible to everyone. As in all learning experiences, once we learn how to do something, it seems so easy. Perhaps many things are much easier than we allow. We have been negatively conditioned by hearing the word "no" over and over again. Let's start using the word "yes" more often.

Sometimes it helps to give ourselves permission to do something. So just go ahead, give yourself permission. Say it out loud, "I give myself permission to enjoy OBE." We can also give each other permission. We believe you can do it; we know you can do it. We have all done it before and will experience the ecstasy again and again.

All you really need do to experience yourself out of body is to love the idea of OBE. Don't try to do an OBE, and don't try not to do an OBE. Just love the idea and it will come to you. It will happen. OBE is like a playful child, spontaneous, natural, joyful and irresistible. OBE will ask you to play when you, too, are a relaxed and playful child.

Affirmations

Are you now beginning to relax more completely and to let go of negative thinking? Have you become more aware of the magic of nature around you, since you have been reading this chapter? As you continue to practice relaxing, you will develop a deeper since of inner peace and tranquility. Your thoughts will become positive and you will begin to understand your interconnectedness with all of life. The following affirmations will help you reinforce the positive information in this chapter.

1. I eagerly create my own sensuous relaxation ritual.

2. My muscles are becoming loose and limp and my mind quiet and peaceful.

3. I allow my healthy, happy child within to emerge and play freely.

4. Day by day, week by week, I am becoming more relaxed, centered and peaceful.

5. Old myths of time urgency and negativity fade into the distance and disappear.

6. I give myself tantalizing invitations for OBE.

7. I am filled with love and I give and receive love in great abundance.

8. I smile inside and out and open my arms to embrace the wonder and glory of OBE.

9. I joyfully anticipate the arrival of OBE again and again.

10. I enjoy communing with nature, knowing that I am a part of all living things.

Selected Readings

Benson, Herbert. *The Relaxation Response*, Avon Books, New York, 1975.

Benson, Herbert. *Beyond the Relaxation Response*, Berkley Books, New York, 1984.

Cousins, Norman. *The Healing Heart,* Avon Books, New York, 1983.

Dass, Ram. *Journey of Awakening: A Meditator's Guidebook*, Bantam Books, New York, 1978.

Dossey, Larry. *Space, Time and Medicine*, Shambhala Publications, Inc., Boulder, Colorado, 1982.

Ellis, Albert. *Reason and Emotion in Psychotherapy*, Lyle Stuart, New York, 1962.

Ellis, Albert and Harper, Robert A. *A New Guide to Rational Living*, Wilshire Book Co., No. Hollywood, California, 1975.

Feuerstein, George. *Yoga: The Technology of Ecstasy*, Jeremy P. Tarcher, Los Angeles, 1989.

Foundation for Inner Peace. *A Course in Miracles,* Combined Volume, Tiburon, California, 1985.

Fromm, Erich. *The Art of Loving*, Harper & Row, New York, 1956.

Keating, Kathleen. *The Hug Therapy Book*, CompCare Publications, Minneapolis, Minnesota, 1983.

Keyes, Jr., Ken. *Handbook to Higher Consciousness*, Living Love Publications, St. Mary, Kentucky, 1975.

LeCron, Leslie M. *Self-Hypnotism: The Technique and Its Use In Daily Living*, Prentice-Hall, Inc., Englewood Cliffs, New Jersey, 1964.

Lindberg, Charles. *The Spirit of St. Louis*, Charles Scribner's Sons, New York, 1953.

Peale, Norman Vincent. *Treasury of Joy and Enthusiasm*, Ballantine Books, New York, 1981.

Stutman, Fred A. *The Doctor's Walking Book*, Ballantine Books, New York, 1979.

Williams, Paul. *Das Energi,* Warner Books, New York, 1973.

4

REAWAKENING DREAMS OF RAPTURE

The Potential

Each of us is creator, director, producer and star in our own dreams. We can create endless dreams of rapture and invite our own special dream lover to fly with us. We can experience any and all feelings and sensations — physical, emotional and spiritual — within our dreams. We can feel everything with a depth of passion that could light a city. And we can bring all of these things into our daily lives. With a little practice, it can be so easy.

We all seek more intimate relationships that allow us to completely merge with our lovers. Yet we want to maintain freedom and express our individuality. Often we have become frustrated with ordinary sex, because it cannot provide total intimacy and complete freedom. But there is another way — there is a limitless intimacy which encourages freedom, establishes perfect communication and creates lingering ecstasy. This profound intimacy lives within each of us and is often awakened during our dreams. Our dreams invite heavenly out-of-body experiences (OBEs) which provide pathways to limitless intimacy.

OBE is one of those wonderful spiritual gifts that allow us to embrace miracles. Yet the out-of-body experience is simply another altered state of consciousness (ASC). We experience many ASCs every day and can easily, automatically shift our awareness to maximize our pleasure. Perhaps one of the most glorious, yet least-appreciated ASCs is the dream state. Dreams are easily accessible to all of us and provide pathways to OBE. Our dreams promote spiritual growth and create limitless ecstasy, especially when we pay attention to them. But dreaming is such a common activity that we tend to overlook its potential for rapture.

We can all direct our dreams; we have all done it before, although we may not be aware of this ability. Perhaps you have had the experience of wanting to sleep late, even though you knew you had an important meeting. So you dreamed you got up, dreamed you got dressed, and dreamed you went to work. Of course, you overslept and missed the meeting. But what if you could really meet someone in a dream? When we are motivated to experience intimacy and ecstasy, we can truly unite with our own special dream lover.

A Sexual Rendezvous

The following transcript describes a dream encounter between lovers who were highly motivated to share intimacy and ecstasy. The speaker is a woman who had married at 18 years of age as a virgin and had remained faithful to her husband.

> *My husband and I had been having serious marital problems for a long time. We had been married for 12 years. I was deeply attracted to another man and began to see him socially. Although I ached for him, I refused to have sex with him. Perhaps it was because of my long marriage commitment or maybe I was just afraid of having sex with him. Perhaps it was some of both. After all, I'd never been with anyone but my husband.*
>
> *I remember it so clearly. One night when my husband did not come home, I was so despondent and lonely. I yearned*

and ached all over for the other man that I loved. I wanted to melt into his arms and make love with him forever. I went to bed asking God to help me overcome my shyness. I prayed for my lover to be sent to me.

About 4:00 a.m., I had a very lucid, detailed dream encounter with my lover. I experienced all the sensuous, romantic feelings, visual images, smells, intimate communications and a very intense orgasm. It was a total, incredible experience of making love. I knew that it was not just a dream; it was a very real ecstasy and my lover was really with me.

The next day I was surprised by an unexpected telephone call from my lover. He told me that he knew I had experienced a "wet" dream about four o'clock in the morning, because he had really been there. He had experienced the same incredible, sexual dream encounter. I felt embarrassed, because of my shyness and lack of sexual experience.

I never had physical sex with this man and do not remember having other sexual dream encounters with him. After about a year, we went our separate ways. I divorced shortly thereafter, and still regret that I declined to pursue that wonderful relationship.

Note that this transcript describes a very real, intense sexual encounter, which was unplanned, yet simultaneously experienced and later verified by the dream lovers. We would find it difficult to classify this as "just a dream." These two lovers obviously had a special relationship which created an open communication channel. This empathic bond allowed them to link their conscious and unconscious mental processes in a very intimate and profound way.

Unconscious Mind, Our Teacher

If we truly want to experience rapture, it is important to integrate conscious and unconscious parts of our minds. Dreams provide communication links between conscious and unconscious processes. When we choose to fully open our dream channel, understanding and pleasure increase rapidly. Our potential as human beings is limitless. There are undeveloped abilities within our unconscious minds that almost defy imagination. But these abilities are only undeveloped from the perspective of the conscious mind. The unconscious mind is already experiencing them. Lucid dreaming is a doorway into these realms. And OBE is a wonderful skill that we can enjoy by recognizing and affirming our unconscious minds.

We tend to identify with our conscious minds to the extent that we may deny the reality of our unconscious minds or consider them irrational. And yet our unconscious minds may very well consider our conscious minds to be asleep or anesthetized to pleasure. When we affirm the wonder and glory of unconscious mind, and finally proclaim that it is alive as we are alive, then we begin to grow in new and more positive directions.

Living in denial of the unconscious mind is like pretending to hate your best friend. Let's remember that unconscious mind is already enjoying OBE and has always enjoyed it. Unconscious mind is a powerful friend and ally. Ask it to show you how to do OBE, then pay attention to what it says. Unconscious mind speaks to you in your dreams. Just listen to your dreams and you will soon remember the bliss of OBE.

Sharing and Learning

We all dream when we sleep, but frequently forget our dreams because they fade so quickly. We tend to ignore our dreams, and take them for granted. But dreams are a very powerful source of insight and can assist all of us in our search for understanding.

We can consciously ask for guidance and receive help from our dreams. Dreams may also provide an enormous wellspring of sexual pleasure.

In Malaysia, the Senoi listen to and learn from their dreams. They discuss their dreams at breakfast every morning. The children begin to share their dreams when first learning to talk, and are encouraged to interact in their dreams in specific ways. The Senoi are taught to advance toward pleasure in their dreams. They interact in their dreams to achieve a positive outcome, confront aggression or danger, and ask for a gift from the aggressor. The gift is then shared with family and friends. For example, when falling in a dream, a Senoi child would learn to convert the act of falling to flying, or follow through by merging with the earth, rather than waking up in fright. Children are also encouraged to ask for help from other individuals in their dreams and to interact with others in positive ways.

The Senoi recognize that young children have a natural ability to dream lucidly and can easily remember their dreams. So they utilize this natural ability and develop it in positive directions. It is helpful to remind ourselves that there is a happy, healthy child that lives within each of us regardless of the specific events of our childhood. When we return to the joyful, healthy child within, we can easily direct our dreams into playful, sensuous adventures.

We have much to learn from the Senoi and their interaction with dreams. Consider the fact that they have zero incidence of neurotic or psychotic behavior, and violence within their society is very rare. Apparently, their dreaming skills affect their entire lifestyle in very positive ways. The Senoi system of dreaming promotes health and encourages dream sex to the point of intense orgasm. Let's learn from the Senoi and develop these wonderful skills. Recall their emphasis on active rather than passive dreaming. We can consciously interact in our dreams like the Senoi. And we can learn from our dreams and receive blessings for our daily lives.

Fascinating Characteristics

Like the Senoi, we have abundant opportunities to create intense dreams of rapture. Did you know that we all dream every night? We each have several periods of dream activity during the course of a normal night's sleep. Our dreams are fascinating ASCs with many interesting characteristics. For example, rapid eye movement (REM) occurs several times during each dream period. REM is a horizontal darting motion of the eyes behind closed eyelids. We can easily observe REM in a sleeping person, because the closed eyelids move when the eyes move behind them. Since the last REM period prior to awakening tends to be the longest and most vivid of the night, it is often the easiest to direct into a delicious adventure.

Ordinary dreams seem so real to us while we are dreaming, that we often do not realize we are dreaming. Our bodies would act out our dreams if there were no built-in safety mechanisms. Most of the time our muscles are disconnected from the brain when we dream. This is called catalepsy. It is not paralysis, but is a type of suspension of voluntary movements. Obviously this has great survival value for a species which used to sleep in trees.

Generally, the autonomic nervous system responds to our dreams, so we have fluctuations in heart rate, respiration and perspiration during sleep. Occasionally dreams will produce shouts, kicks and punches. More often, our dreams stimulate erection, lubrication and orgasm. Events such as sleep walking are somewhat rare although we've all heard an amusing story or two. We believe our dreams are perfectly real while in a dream, so real that our bodies may react to the dream the same way they react to waking events. We are active but not aware that we are dreaming. Such is an ordinary dream, as contrasted with a lucid dream.

Ordinary dreams must be recalled very quickly upon awakening or they tend to fade before we can record them. If we think of other things or if more than ten minutes has elapsed since the end of REM, then recall is poor. However if we experience a lucid dream, we may remember it forever, because our conscious and unconscious processes are interacting so effectively in a lucid dream.

We can all enjoy our natural ability to dream lucidly. Lucid dreaming is just like being awake in a dream. It is exhilarating and fun. Can you remember being in control of a particular dream and thinking how pleasantly different this type of dreaming was? That was a lucid dream. We can increase our skill at lucid dreaming by simply paying more attention to our ordinary dreams. We begin by recalling our dreams when we awaken.

Enhancing Dream Recall

When falling asleep we can enhance dream recall by saying to ourselves, "I will remember my dreams tonight." We can also suggest topics for our dreams or ask for clarification of a previous dream. In order to explicitly and directly influence dream content, it helps to develop the skill of lucid dreaming. When we are lucid within a dream, we are aware that we are dreaming while we are dreaming. During lucid dreams, we can make positive choices, affect the outcome of the dream or create a sensuous rendezvous with our dream lover.

An excellent means of improving our dream recall is to start a dream journal. We can write in a notebook or speak into a tape recorder for a few minutes each morning. Some of us like to set our alarms a few minutes early when keeping a dream journal. Others prefer to awake naturally, keeping the eyes closed, and shifting the bodies slowly to different positions in bed to recall the dreams we had while asleep in each of those positions. Some of us write in the dark, while others get up after a few moments of silent recall and write at a desk. It is often helpful to have a friend awaken us at the moment rapid eye movement stops. You may want to experiment to see what works best for you. But above all, avoid being compulsive or perfectionistic; you want to maintain an attitude of curious adventure, not drudgery.

Dream recall promotes lucid dreaming. In order to become skilled at lucid dreaming, we need only show a sincere interest in our dreams. Obviously lucid dreaming can be very exciting and rewarding, vastly more so than ordinary dreaming. And as we observe our ordinary dreams, we automatically increase our skill at recognizing when we are dreaming. At the moment we realize we are dreaming, we have the power to direct the dream and to make it lucid.

We know that each dream we record in our dream journals contains a gift from our unconscious minds. We can learn to recognize and cherish these gifts. Sometimes the gift is simply pleasure which allows us to carry forth happiness and love into our daily lives. Perhaps the simplest gifts are the best.

Unconscious mind is limitless and contains incredibly vast amounts of information. It is also a very effective teacher. It uses a language of symbols that have personal meaning for us and for those who know us well. We often find it helpful to ask close friends to read parts of our dream journal and give their interpretations. And when we share the sensuality of our dreams, they become even more erotic and pleasurable.

Awakening and Entering a Dream

In the twilight sleep just before awakening, it is easy to re-enter a dream and retain a waking consciousness. Then we know that we are dreaming even though everything appears vividly real. Once lucid, we have the power to make a dream super-real: colors more vibrant, trees more alive, skies deeper and so forth. There really are no limits. Think about this for a moment. Let us say that someone offered to show us a new movie-making technology that involved all the senses, not just sight and sound. Would we be willing to learn how to enjoy this new technology?

It is surprisingly easy for each of us to develop our innate ability to attain the lucid dream ASC. It does not take years of meditation or nights strapped to an EEG in a dream lab. We each know that we can alter dreams when we consider how often daily events influence our dreams. For example, people we see during the day often re-appear in our dreams the same night. A lucid dreamer can influence his dream while in the dream.

What if you woke up in a dream? Well, that is exactly what lucid dreaming is like. It's as though the experience becomes an exploration of alternate realities. Who is to say we don't wake up into a different dream every day anyway? Certainly each of us perceives things a bit differently from the next person. Which perception is more real? Let's choose to perceive more intimacy and ecstasy.

Some things that we only do rarely in a waking state are much easier to do in a dream. Did you know that dream telepathy really happens? Most of us are aware that the content of dreams can be influenced by light and sound within a sleeper's bedroom. For example, if we observe REM in a sleeper and describe a painting during REM, then features of the painting will most likely be incorporated into the dream. Likewise, if we simply relax and focus on the painting, with the intent of sharing it telepathically with the dreamer, then the dream will often contain unmistakable associations with the painting. Do you find this difficult to believe? Dream telepathy such as this has been repeatedly verified in strict laboratory conditions.

Did you ever have a premonition in the form of a dream? Did someone ever call to you in a dream that seemed much more than a dream? Did you know that you can meet people in your dreams, and that dreams can be real? Yes, two individuals can share the same dream. Think about this for a moment. If two independent observers perceive the same thing, doesn't that make it real?

Mahayana Buddhists practice lucid dreaming and are able to enter others' dreams at will. People of like mind sometimes even link unintentionally. In *Way of the White Clouds*, Lama Govinda visited the Abbot of Lachen in Tibet. Arriving late one evening, he went directly to bed without first meeting the Abbot. However, at the moment of falling asleep, Govinda suddenly found his mind directly linked to the Abbot's and experienced the Abbot's exact thoughts and feelings. Wouldn't it be wonderful if you could do this with a close friend? Well, you can, and you don't have to be an abbot either.

When we understand that lucid dreaming is just another ASC, then we know that we can create a type of lucid dream when we are awake. The state of lucid dreaming may be entered easily by individuals who practice for a few nights. It may appear to a casual observer that we are unconscious whenever we are in the lucid dream state or in any of a number of other ASCs. For example, hypnosis is often thought of as sleep and may even be referred to as sleep by the hypnotist. But we know that hypnosis is definitely not sleep. Meditative states are not at all like sleep either, except in outward appearance. Hypnosis and meditation are both avenues to the lucid dream state and may be easier routes than sleep for individuals already trained in their use. It may be effective to have a hypnotist induce a waking dream or give a post-hypnotic suggestion to become lucid in a dream.

Dream Lovers

The following vignette is an example of a hypnotically induced encounter with a dream lover. Note the total intimacy, sensuality and freedom in this woman's experience.

> *It was spring and we met in the mountains. He has the most intense, beautiful blue eyes. And it's exceptional because he's not fair-skinned or blond or what you normally would consider with blue eyes. He's dark with those blue, blue eyes. His touch is so gentle. He touches like most men don't*

know how to touch. He's not rough. He's so gentle, very gentle. And he knows all the right places to touch.

He's so beautiful and I'm beautiful. There are no more surgical scars on my body — they're all gone. I'm young and thin and beautiful again and all the surgical scars are gone. We are completely nude, all the time always nude. There are no clothes to bind us or hold us back. It isn't necessary to have clothes to be warm, or comfortable or socially acceptable. We don't have to worry about how we look, because we're just so beautiful. You see, we are perfect and beautiful without clothes or make-up or working at it. We have a perfect climate and never have to put on clothes, nothing to put on or take off.

The moon came out and we got on a boat and rowed across a beautiful lake to this serene waterfall. We sat by the waterfall and listened to the sounds of the waterfall. We just watched the reflection of the moon on the water and listened. We didn't talk, but we could sense each other's deepest feelings and thoughts. Words were unnecessary. Our communication was automatic and perfect — telepathic, I guess. We just knew every thought and feeling instantly and automatically.

When we make love, we hold each other so close and yet the pressure doesn't hurt. It's so gentle, so close. I've never been so close before. It's difficult to explain. Just lying in the hammock and swinging back and forth is so wonderful. Everything is so right, so wonderful.

The shared intimacy and sexual bonding in this dream encounter were intense. Note that the lovers were naturally beautiful and free from clothes and other restrictions. Sometimes we have all felt negative about our physical bodies, so it is nice to know we are all beautiful in our divine spiritual forms. Also note this couple's telepathic communication, with all thoughts and feelings perceived instantly and perfectly. How wonderful it would be to savor this kind of intimacy with your own special dream lover tonight!

Everyone has a dream lover, a true starmate. You can meet your starmate in a dream. Tantric yoga calls this dream mate the saha-dharmini. You can experience limitless passion with your starmate in a lucid, real dream whenever you choose. You need not be asleep. Once we develop the ability to dream lucidly, we discover that what we thought was everyday life in this world is only a small corner of the universe available to us at each moment. Our everyday world is real and valid, but is only the tip of the iceberg. By altering our consciousness we can perceive different aspects of reality. Just as the spectrum of light extends far beyond the colors we are able to perceive with the naked eye, so too does all of reality extend far beyond our ordinary awareness. Perhaps your starmate is waiting just at the edge of your vision at this very moment.

Our dream adventures are truly limitless. We can enjoy bathing in moonbeams on a secluded tropical beach or making love in a luxurious hotel suite that is furnished with sensuous delights. We can share a flirtatious lunch at a sidewalk cafe in Paris or waltz through the streets of Venice. We can fly hand-in-hand over the trees, float on a cloud and frolic with the birds. We can choose ecstasy again and again. In what sensuous places will you choose to meet your dream lover tonight?

We can all easily create special daydreams and nightdreams. There are any number of rich images we can focus on while lying in bed. For example, imagine standing on a hill under the stars on a beautiful summer night. As you gaze into the starry heavens, you can almost cup your hands behind the stars and pull them down to you. Now allow a warm breeze to lift you up into the sky, so you can enjoy the ecstasy of flying free.

Flying Free

Many human activities are motivated by a desire to fly free. Consider snow skiing, sky diving, soaring, surfing, skating and bicycling. Many of us often dream of flying like a bird. Actually, flying dreams are often OBEs. And lucid dreaming is significantly related to OBE. Although OBE may begin as a dream, it is not an ordinary dream, as anyone who has been there can tell you. OBE has the characteristic of lucidity. In fact the distinction between OBE and lucid dreaming may only be semantic. That is, it really doesn't matter what we call this very pleasant state. It is enough to know that we can indeed fly while in this ASC.

Here is a typical account of one person's recollection of his flying dreams. If you survey several people at random, you may find that flying dreams are quite similar from one person to the next.

> *I associate flying with birds. I remember believing I could fly without wings and that I could fly without an airplane. Later on in life I thought how childlike and irrational that was — how really stupid it was. I remember we were laughing about this when we saw a movie about the history of aviation, especially when they showed some of that wonderful footage of all the early people who were trying to develop a technique for flying. They would strap bird's wings on their arms, then jump off barns and sometimes kill themselves. They did the strangest things, yet some of those people seemed to have the same kind of sense I had about flying. I knew I didn't need this huge airplane to fly in.*
>
> *In terms of evolution, we can propose that mankind has always been fascinated with flying. I wish now that I could see the movie on the history of aviation again. It's just wonderful. Many of them wanted to fly by simply spreading their arms and flying. It also reminds me of parasailing, too, which is kind of flying on the wind currents with very little*

apparatus. That's the physical realm of flying I remember as a child. I knew I could fly and believed very deeply that I did fly.

It seemed very curious and a little disappointing that I only would fly at nighttime. When I went to sleep, I entered this magical world and I could somehow then fly — something I couldn't do when I was awake and I was rather envious about that. I called them dreams. Now I believe that I was in fact leaving my body as a young child and did so for years. I did childlike things, fun things when I was out of my body.

My parents were rather serious people and there was not a lot of laughter or play. There was play during some periods, but you were expected to grow up pretty fast. I remember loving the sensation of flying in my dreams. It was such an exhilarating feeling. My favorite thing was to wait — be drifting along, standing or floating just a short way off the ground — and wait for a gust of wind. Then I would sort of leap or float up into the wind and ride the wind currents. I would just fly over acres and acres. I loved flying over treetops with the wind and over buildings and sort of dipping and flying up and down. It was just a very, very exhilarating feeling, so those flying dreams were very important to me.

It is interesting how common they are, flying dreams. I have talked to so many people who have flying dreams. My flying dreams are so powerful that I feel wonderful for days afterwards. The feeling lingers, so it isn't like I need to fly or even want to fly particularly every night, although sometimes flying occurs on successive nights. It always makes my body feel so good. And also, I experience a kind of absence of worry, which was important when I was a child, because I was kind of a serious child who was prone to worry. I was always happy and up for days after flying.

Flying dreams are extremely arousing. Freud suggested that flying in dreams signified a desire to have sex. Lucid dream research supports the concept that flying in a dream can be a form of sexual foreplay. In the dream labs, flying dreams have been associated with increased blood flow to the sexual organs, for example. Flying is a common mode of travel in an OBE and a wonderful prelude to sexual dream encounters.

The Joy of Dream Sex

Lucid sexual dreams are especially intense experiences. Dream orgasms can be infinitely more satisfying than physically-stimulated orgasms. This is partly because we avoid overexertion in dream sex. But the superiority of dream sex derives mainly from the increased freedom we all have in our dreams. We can easily transcend mortal boundaries and limits within a dream.

It is easy to influence our dreams with a taped message timed to play during a probable REM period of sleep. Since the longest REM period is just before waking, we often set a timer to activate the tape player 30 minutes to an hour before our normal waking time. When you experiment with this technique, you may be amazed with your success. If you find that the onset of the tape player has jolted you out of the dream, simply reduce the volume next time.

If two people listen to the same tape while going to sleep, it is easy for them to share the same dream simultaneously. This is an extremely exciting experience. Two people can be together in a single dream, sharing a wonderfully intimate experience. A shared lucid dream is indescribably pleasurable and goes far beyond the scope of an ordinary dream. It involves dream telepathy. Can you imagine what this kind of sharing is like? We can each experience a lovers' paradise of limitless ecstasy, an ecstasy that some people are enjoying right now.

We have designed a special dream technique which will allow you to experience the rapture. Feel free to enjoy it alone or share it with a lover. It is OK if you do not already have a lover. Soon you will dance in starlight with your own special dream lover. The sensations which you experience with this technique may be different from anything that you have ever felt before. Afterwards, you may find that your experience is indescribable.

Slowly prepare for a date with your special dream lover. Enjoy a warm, leisurely bubble bath or shower. Burn incense and play romantic music. Dress in special, sensuous clothing and wear your favorite cologne. Put special sheets or blankets on your bed. Prepare yourself, your room and your bed for an incomparable dream of rapture.

When you are ready for sleep, turn on the tape player or set the timer to activate the tape player approximately 45 minutes before your normal waking time. Position yourself comfortably in your bed, pull the covers up and fluff your pillow. Allow yourself to become snugly warm. Focus your mind on positive thoughts and images, so that all the cares of the day are far, far away. Relax and allow yourself to drift into a natural sleep.

You may record the following dialogue for playback in your sleep. You may find it effective to play while falling asleep or just before awakening. Refer to the appendix for instructions on how to record your own tape, or order professionally recorded tapes from the publisher. Once you learn to share a dream with your special lover, you will no longer need the tape player.

> You are so relaxed and peaceful, drifting into a dreamy twilight sleep. All around you there's a beautiful sense of velvet darkness, caressing you. It feels so good, so peaceful — drifting and floating. Feel yourself drifting into the most delicious dream. Your body is relaxed, tingling. And you may feel a sinking sensation or a heaviness as you enter this starlit dream world.
>
> Now begin to feel the gentle breeze on your face. You are driving in your favorite automobile, the one you have always wanted to own. It's as though you are one with

the car, as it responds perfectly to your every move. You are driving slowly along a gently winding road in the mountains. You feel an indescribable kind of freedom — freedom like you have never felt before.

It's late afternoon on a beautiful autumn day and the mountains and valleys are alive with vibrant colors of red, yellow and orange. You are fascinated by the sun-kissed leaves blowing in the wind — golden leaves dancing in concentric patterns along the road in front of you. In the distance, the white patches of snow are sprinkled on mountain tops like powdered-sugar frosting.

The images of beauty all around you create beautiful feelings deep inside of you. You are beautiful like the mountains and valleys and you are instinctively connected to them. Each free, gentle and easy breath you take promotes peace and tranquility — mind, body and spirit in perfect balance and harmony.

You feel an eager sense of anticipation beginning to wash over you now. There's a special excitement stirring deep within the love center of your soul. You are nearing that majestic pine tree which overlooks the trail leading to your cabin. How wonderful it is to return to your own special haven in the mountains! It's such a delightful sanctuary filled with beauty, joy and ecstasy beyond compare. At long last, the love of your life is just a heartbeat away.

As you park the car and step outside, you smell the refreshing scent of pine and cedar drifting in the clean mountain air. You begin to walk the short trail leading to the cabin, listening to the leaves crunching beneath your feet and longing for the arms which will soon embrace you. In a moment, you will be blessed with the love for which you have always yearned.

Now you smell smoke from the glowing fireplace floating gently on the breeze. You look at the door of the cabin and know that you are truly home at last. Suddenly the door is opened and you gaze into those misty eyes overflowing with love. As you look into the beautiful eyes of your dream lover, you see reflections of your own soul. For an instant, you yearn to walk into those eyes, close the lids behind you and shut out the world.

In a heartbeat, you are firmly embraced by those warm, gentle arms — holding, stroking, caressing you. You are surrounded by love, so much love. You are kissing — warm, sugary kisses that never end. Soft, wet kisses are spreading all over your body creating waves of ecstasy.

Stretch out on that soft fur rug in front of the fireplace. The soft fur and the warm glow of the fire feel so good on your nude body. There's magic in the hands that love you more with each touch and excite every cell in your body. You have that indescribable feeling that you get just before orgasm. It's so wonderful, making love the way you always dreamed it could be. You can feel the total merging of your bodies until it is impossible to know where one begins and the other ends. You are one, inseparable — a swirling vortex of ecstasy.

All your sexual fantasies can now be realities. And there is more — beyond your wildest fantasy. You will enjoy endless waves of orgasms flowing over your entire body. You can stay in this continual state of orgasm, drifting into a blissful rapture for as long as you wish.

You can direct your dream and create any delicious delights that you desire. Perhaps you will dance nude under a skylight glowing with a billion stars. Or you may relish a candlelight dinner in a hottub on the balcony. You may share ecstasy in a rocking chair or sway gently together in a hammock. You have limitless possibilities for creating exquisite dreams of rapture.

It is so wonderful to be with your dream lover. And you can fly together any night you choose. Your dreams will be so lucid that you can always direct them into flights of ecstasy. You can return to your own special cabin in the mountains or journey to any other sensuous place whenever you wish. You will always receive a gift in your dreams and all your dreams will be positive adventures. When you awaken from this dream, you will feel a room full of smiles that will linger with you for days and days.

Affirmations

You have now become more aware of your innate process of dreaming and are beginning to develop your potential for creating and directing dreams of rapture. As you continue to awaken into your dreams, you will develop new understanding and insight. Simply by continuing to expand your awareness, you will create spiritual bonds with other people and begin to share the ecstasy of limitless intimacy.

1. I am spiritually, sexually alive in my dreams.

2. I can create endless dreams of rapture and fly starlit pathways to OBE.

3. My dreams are delightful productions of my creative life force.

4. I joyfully remember my dreams and discover precious jewels of insight within them.

5. I dream in vibrant colors, delectable tastes, delicious scents and sensuous textures.

6. Being aware in a dream is an easy and wonderful opportunity for adventure and ecstasy.

7. The freedom within a dream is boundless and allows me to create a heavenly pleasure dome.

8. I open my heart and invite my own special dream lover to fly with me.

9. When I meet my dream lover, we share perfect, complete understanding and sex beyond compare.

10. When I keep my eyes closed upon awakening, I can recall my dream scene by scene in all its luscious detail.

Selected Readings

Bandler, Richard and Grindler, John. *The Structure of Magic*, Science and Behavior Books, Palo Alto, California, 1975.

Bach, Richard. *Jonathan Livingston Seagull*, Avon Books, New York, 1970.

Bryant, Dorothy. *The Kin of Ata are Waiting for You*, Random House, New York, 1971.

Garfield, Patricia. *Creative Dreaming*, Ballantine, New York, 1974.

Garfield, Patricia. *Pathway to Ecstasy*, Holt, Rhinehart and Winston, New York, 1974.

Garrison, Omar. *Tantra: the Yoga of Sex*, Julian Press, New York, 1964.

Govinda, Lama Anagarika. *The Way of the White Clouds*, Shambala, Berkeley, 1970.

LaBerge, Stephen. *Lucid Dreaming*, Ballantine, New York, 1985.

Mitchell, Janet Lee. *Out-of-Body Experiences: A Handbook*, Ballantine Books, New York, 1981.

Ryback, David. *Dreams That Come True*, Doubleday, New York, 1974.

Stack, Richard. *Out-of-Body Adventures: 30 Days to the Most Exciting Experience of Your Life*, Contemporary Books, New York, 1988.

Ullman and Krippner. *Dream Telepathy,* Penguin Books, Baltimore, Maryland, 1973.

5

VISUALIZING PATHWAYS TO OBS

The Pathways

We are all spiritual beings — filled with divine sexual energy. But we have just begun to affirm how wonderful we really are. If we open our eyes a little wider, we can see reality and find our guiding light. At this very moment, we are in the process of creating a paradise which blesses us with abundant pathways to ecstasy.

SAWNKI (sex as we now know it) is a path to ecstasy, but it is a limited trail with many obstacles and detours. When we affirm our spirituality and allow our awareness to expand and flow freely, we can create a new kind of ecstasy — an intense, lingering ecstasy that teaches us to love ourselves and others unconditionally. Through a process of spiritual bonding, we can share the ultimate intimacy, a merging of souls. Can you imagine yourself and your lover as dancing laser lights, harmonizing and blending in an endless orgasmic fusion?

The process of spiritual bonding often begins with relaxation. Relaxation is an easy, magical path to ecstasy which we can all learn. Simply by becoming quiet, still and centered we invite spontaneous out-of-body experiences. When we relax with faith and return to the joyful child within, then we are prepared for miracles. Let's remember that miracles happen when we believe in them and when we are ready to accept them.

In reality, there are many miracles inside of us, all around us and throughout our universe. Our nightdreams and daydreams are miracles which illuminate angelic pathways to new worlds. It is so easy to fly these starlit pathways by simply observing and remembering our dreams. We can also create and savor endless flights of rapture with our own special starmates. And did you know that a sensuous starflight can become a reality when we imagine it vividly and intensely? We begin by simply relaxing and increasing our faith.

All pathways lead us back to the Garden of Eden. But of course, we have never really left the garden. It's just that our vision has become blurred and we have become disoriented. Actually we can see farther and more clearly than we realize. Did you know that African bushmen named the four largest moons of Jupiter long before Galileo invented the telescope? Perhaps we really can see forever. And to journey back to paradise, all we need do is focus our vision and expand our awareness.

Our Life Force

If we expand our vision, what do we see? We see the wonder and glory of life — life filled with pure, abundant sexual energy. What is sexual energy? It is our power source, our life force. It is the thread that creates life and links us with everything in the universe. Sexual energy is divinely spiritual. When we are fully human, we are spiritually and sexually alive.

Our divine sexuality is our link to the universe, to all generations past and future; it is our special link to other human beings. As a race and as individuals, we can now expand to embrace a spiritual/physical harmony. We can access the free-flowing sexual energy or life force of the universe, which accepts no boundaries and chooses no limits. We as individuals have a choice — accept smallness, or embrace the universe. And we make this choice every moment of our lives.

We are all looking for a means of understanding and affirming ourselves. As a race we are evolving very rapidly now into a state of expanded awareness and part of this next big evolutionary step is spiritual sex, the great fulfillment. What is spiritual sex? It is a new, beautiful way of loving and sharing which allows us to experience ecstasy beyond belief. It is a merging of souls without loss of freedom, a deeper intimacy with perfect communication and lingering satisfaction. With spiritual sex, we journey beyond physical limitations and learn the true meaning of unconditional love.

Out-of-Body Sex

Spiritual sex is often called out-of-body sex or OBS. It can be defined as a shared out-of-body experience between two or more spirits or souls. And the out-of body experience (OBE) is just an alteration or expansion of consciousness, a very normal human activity. There are many techniques for creating an OBE, so we are all free to choose our favorite ones. Out-of-body sex can be experienced by any motivated individual. Simply by relaxing and expanding our perceptions, we can alter our consciousness and extend awareness into the spiritual realm. When we invite another person to join us in this spiritual realm, we can share a vivid, very real ecstasy that allows us to unite in a way which reveals that all the worries of SAWNKI are trivial, amusing and even silly.

Sex as we now know it (SAWNKI) can be nice, sometimes even awe-inspiring; it almost gets us there, but it is just a taste, a shadow of OBS. SAWNKI is like the reflection of the moon on the surface of a lake. When the lake is calm, the image is almost indistinguishable from the real thing. But when the waters are disturbed, the image is distorted. SAWNKI at its best is a distorted image of OBS, because even when the image is clear, the viewer tends to miss the point entirely. And that point is the fact that what we see on the lake is simply sunlight twice removed. In contrast, the OBS experience is like being able to soar directly into the sun itself.

OBS is a magical way of sharing the very essence of ourselves with another person. It is a spiritual experience that is also very sexual and so pleasurable. Sometimes OBS is accompanied by an intense physical orgasm or may occur during physical sex. But OBS is more than physical sex, much more. It is indescribable with mere words and has to be experienced to be understood. When we experience OBS, we begin to form spiritual bonds with other people. It is this process of spiritual bonding which introduces us to the bliss of limitless intimacy.

To enjoy the bliss of limitless intimacy, we need only learn to create and share out-of-body experiences. OBEs occur most frequently during relaxation, visualization and lucid dreaming. We have already learned to relax into peaceful expectations and to observe dreams of rapture. To advance from OBE to OBS, it is helpful to increase our visualization skills.

Shifting Perceptions

To increase our visualization skills, we want to turn off our analytical left brains and activate our creative right brains. We can begin to free our imaginations by learning to create and move perceptual images. Visual fixation techniques can help train us to make a perceptual jump from one point of observation to another. Stare at each of the figures presented below for a few moments. You may find it helpful to cover all but one of the figures, so that your focus is more intense.

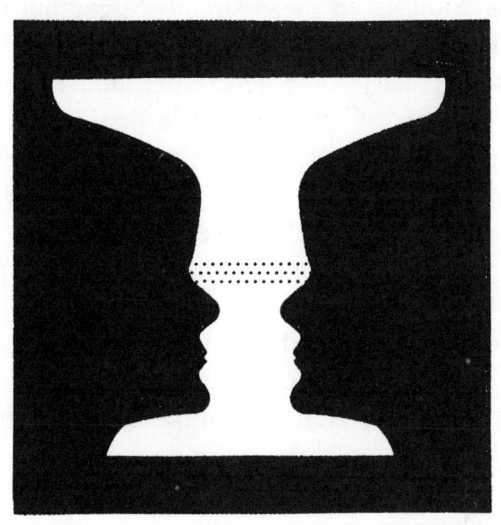

Notice how easily these shapes seem to move as you stare at them. Shifting awareness during an OBE is similar to these types of perceptual jumps. Continue practicing with these figures until you can intentionally induce the perceptual jumps by merely blinking your eyes. For additional practice, feel free to use your own favorite drawings or abstract pictures.

When you have mastered these simple perceptual techniques, you will be prepared for the shifts in awareness which occur during OBEs. Actually some perceptual jumps appear to be a limited type of OBE. Can you believe that such a wonderful skill can be so easy? Of course we are reluctant to believe that a cherished skill could be so easy. We are afraid to accept simplicity, so we imagine that it is very difficult and sometimes discount our OBEs by defining them as "quirks" of perception. Our OBEs may be "quirks" of perception, but these "quirks" of perception may indicate a shift of awareness to a point outside our bodies. Let's remind ourselves that there really is no evidence that awareness is located in the body, the brain or any one particular place.

A Perceptual Shift Into OBE

The following transcript describes an OBE which occurred spontaneously with a sudden shift in perception. Note that this individual was simply relaxing and practicing self-hypnosis by staring at an abstract picture.

> *This was one of my very first OBEs. I was attending college working on a degree in psychology. One day I was practicing self-hypnosis using a fixation technique. I was lying on my back, staring at an abstract art painting. So of course, I had my eyes open. I was staring at the painting just watching the movement of colors and patterns. I suddenly felt this shift in consciousness, a visual shift or a shift in my mind. Suddenly I became aware that I was floating out of my body. I looked down and saw my body lying there looking at the picture. Then I had a moment of panic. I remember thinking, "Oh, dear, this is not supposed to be happening."*
>
> *I couldn't believe what was happening. I was a very dedicated scientist at the time and quite critical of hypnosis. I rejected such experiences as mere superstition. When I looked down at my body, it really frightened me. During that*

period of my life, I was very data oriented and had no conscious awareness that I had been doing OBEs. I was a very strict behavioral scientist.

Anyway it scared me so badly that I immediately returned to my body and awakened with a shock, like an electric shock. This was a very, very real experience, but somehow I managed to dismiss it and tried to forget about it. I believed that it was weird and dangerous or maybe a dream. However a part of me, deep inside, always knew it was real. For a long time afterwards, I set myself up to prevent this spontaneous type of OBE from happening again.

It is interesting to note how quickly we can discount experience in the name of science. What we have labeled "science" has made many great contributions to our lives. But sometimes we have blocked our vision and limited our perceptions in the name of science. At one point in history, our science told us that the world was flat and we believed it, even though we could see the curvature as boats sailed over the horizon. We have falsely believed that science is the only vision of reality. But this "reality" is simply what we see when we narrow or restrict our awareness. So it is very important to continue opening our perceptions and expanding our awareness.

Seeing Through Closed Eyes

Here is an easy exercise which will help expand your awareness and invite glorious OBEs. Begin by selecting a room with a blank wall. Remove all objects which are near the wall. Place two simple objects on a table in front of the wall. Adjust the lighting and prepare your environment in a way that pleases you. Place a comfortable chair five to ten feet from the table. Sit in the chair, clear your inner space and relax your muscles.

Stare at one object, until you memorize everything about it. Now do the same for the other object. Then allow your gaze to jump back and forth between the two objects. Close your eyes and visualize first one object and then the other one. Create the objects in exquisite detail in your mind's eye. Allow your perception to jump back and forth between the two objects. You may open your eyes and stare at the objects any time you wish to reinforce your perception. Practice seeing the objects through your closed eyelids. Just relax and let it happen.

You may suddenly find that you have forgotten whether your eyes are open or closed. Also you may find that you are seeing the room quite vividly with your eyes closed. When this occurs, move your perceptual vantage point to a different angle of viewing. For example, look at the objects from behind or from above. This is a dynamic OBE and gives you an effective stepping stone to the more advanced OBS.

As soon as you become aware of perceptual shifts, give yourself permission to leave your body. You may then visualize yourself standing up or floating out of your body. See yourself from a position that is independent of the body. Note that the room may appear brighter than before or your vision may seem more lucid. Enjoy whatever you perceive and let yourself begin to feel the ecstasy which accompanies an OBE.

Abundant Opportunities

Here is another easy exercise that invites OBEs. Find a corner of a room free of paintings and other objects on the walls and ceiling. Lie flat on your back with your head in the corner and feet toward the middle of the room. Look up at the ceiling and imagine you are looking down at the floor. Continue fixating on the ceiling until you can allow your awareness to shift freely. Imagine a floating sensation, as though you were floating on a raft in a warm, shallow pool. Then give yourself permission to float out of your body. Just relax and know that you will float comfortably without falling. Practice this technique several times. Your skill level will increase automatically each time you practice this exercise.

We have abundant opportunities to enjoy OBEs. There are limitless visual fixation techniques which provide wonderful paths to OBEs. So each of us can choose the ones which we find most pleasurable. We often enjoy fixating on a tiny light in a dark room, a twinkling star in the sky, a pretty rosebud or a blue circle. We allow the lights to move, the circle to spin, or the rosebud to open into a beautiful flower of love.

While we are fixating, we practice the perceptual jump experience. This allows us to transfer our consciousness to an object and to develop a sense of merging with the object. We want our identification with the object to be so complete that we experience ourselves as one with the object. Then we can project our consciousness totally away from the body. We want to perceive and think from different spots in the room. When we look back at our bodies, then we truly know the wonder and glory of human freedom.

Many of us are already quite skilled with visual fixation. Recall the mirror/love exercise in Chapter Three. Feel free to modify or expand this exercise to please yourself. For example, practice transferring awareness back and forth between your body and your mirror image. Then move your awareness out into the space between your body and the mirror. Or perhaps you will want to tape a picture of a dream lover on the mirror, so that you can see the reflection of your lover in the middle of your own reflection. Do you love the idea of seeing this beautiful image inside of you? This simulates OBS and will help you mentally prepare for the indescribable merging of spirits.

Sharing Paths to Ecstasy

Visual fixation techniques may be practiced alone or with a partner. If they are shared with a partner, communication should be non-verbal for a significant period of time. When these techniques are shared with a lover, there is an automatic increase in the sensuality of the experience.

We have all discovered that SAWNKI can be a path to ecstasy. But did you know that we can combine SAWNKI with projecting our awareness to create a special type of OBS? Simply by standing outside of our bodies, we can watch ourselves in the rapture of lovemaking. We can view the experience from all kinds of new and exciting angles and perspectives. Of course, we want to avoid monitoring, analyzing and evaluating. For when we are lost in perceiving and feeling, SAWNKI can become OBS. Then we are blessed with the ecstatic intimacy for which we have always yearned.

The following technique is an advanced visual fixation which some of us prefer to do alone, while others choose to invite a partner. Place two chairs a few feet from each other. Sit in one chair and stare at the other one. As you relax and become centered, transfer your awareness to the other chair. Experience yourself sitting in the other chair looking back at your body. You may also stand out of your body by simply imaging a forward and upward movement of your ethereal spirit. If you are sharing this experience with a partner, then stand out of your body and invite your partner to join you in a sensuous dance. If you have ever enjoyed dancing with someone you love, then you have an indescribably delicious experience awaiting you!

Flying Free

One of the most wonderful benefits of practicing visual fixation is that practice increases the occurrence of spontaneous OBEs. So just before going to sleep some evening, you may suddenly find yourself standing at the foot of the bed looking at your body. Or when awakening some morning, you may find that you are floating and looking at the ceiling from a few inches away. Or perhaps you'll notice that you are seeing clearly with your eyes closed. When these events occur, you may truly take flight and journey wherever your heart desires.

If we are to fly free, then it is important to avoid analyzing, intellectualizing, judging and monitoring. For as soon as we begin to analyze the experience, we are pulled back into our bodies. We want to suspend analytical processes and become immersed in feeling, intuiting and perceiving. Sometimes we analyze and monitor because we are afraid. Fear and anxiety can block OBE. But we can alleviate fear of OBE when we realize that our soul, spirit, astral projection or whatever we care to call it, is no more than our own consciousness operating in a relaxed, receptive, very natural mode. As with most joyful new things, fears are quickly dismissed in the bliss of the experience.

The initial fear associated with OBE is easily overcome when its origins are understood. There is a tendency to associate OBE with death because the human spirit may be thought of as a ghost. We fear that the body will die if our consciousness is directed away from it. But the body's autonomic systems maintain normal bodily functions during all kinds of changes in perception and awareness. So if there is a problem or discomfort during sleep, dreaming or OBE (for example, an arm falls asleep), we will wake up, stop dreaming, or re-focus our perceptions.

We are no more vulnerable when doing OBE than we are when asleep. But keep in mind that OBE is not sleep. Actually, ordinary consciousness seems like sleep when compared to OBE. True, the body is in a profoundly relaxed state and may appear to be asleep during OBE, but consciousness is very aware, very awake and thrillingly alive.

Preferred Sensory Modalities

Visual fixation techniques awaken our consciousness and provide pathways to OBE and OBS. Fixation techniques are simply a way of focusing our perceptions, until we are able to expand our awareness beyond old, self-imposed limits. Although we usually practice visual fixation, we can also fixate using any of our other senses. For example, we enjoy fixating on the sounds of music or rain and the smell of incense. And fixating on the perception of gentle touch and movement are often wonderful paths to OBS.

Many of us seem to have a dominant or preferred sensory modality, which can be discovered by careful observation. This preference may be indicated by statements like "I hear what you're saying" (auditory), or "I see what you mean" (visual). We have found it helpful to practice with different techniques to discover which sensory modalities work best for us. Often the preferred sensory modality is the one which brings us the highest degree of pleasure.

Fixation techniques which focus multiple senses simultaneously are powerful pathways to OBS. One of our favorites is drifting on a sailboat on a warm spring day. Immediately we relish the warmth of the sun and the coolness of the breeze on our bare skin. Then we are automatically drawn to fixate on the floating, rocking motion of the boat. At the same time, our eyes are captivated by sunlight sparkling across the surface of the water or fluffy, white clouds drifting against a clear blue sky. When we share a sensuous massage, then the ultimate ecstasy is just a sparkle away.

Opportunities for multiple sensory fixation are limited only by our imagination. When we free our creativity, then our imagination is indeed limitless. Some of our favorite delights have been created while relaxing at the beach, sitting on a mountain top, lying in a hammock, soaking in a hot tub, strolling beside a babbling stream, sitting by a waterfall, flying in a sailplane, sharing a picnic lunch and looking at the city lights from a tall building. Which sensuous places will you choose to focus your perceptions and expand your awareness?

Reactivating Childhood Skills

Sometimes we believe that it is difficult to travel to our favorite places for relaxation and creative expansion. But it is really very, very easy. We can travel to the most beautiful, sensuous places in the world — and beyond — whenever we choose. As children, we all enjoyed active imaginations and rich fantasy experiences. When we reactivate our natural childhood abilities of imagery and fantasy, we can experience mental journeys into ecstasy.

Imagination and fantasy are fixation techniques which create vivid perceptual images and allow us to focus and move our awareness. They also provide extremely effective pathways to OBS. It is important to understand that the word "fantasy" is sometimes a misnomer used to label something we don't understand. Images and fantasies are simply forms of mental activity that can stimulate and create very real experiences.

Here is a quick way to experience the "real-ness" of imagery/fantasy. Close your eyes and imagine that you are holding a fresh lemon in your hand. Examine it carefully looking at the shape, design and vivid yellow color. Rub it between your hands, feel the surface texture, the firmness and curved form. Place it on a cutting board and cut the lemon in half. Listen to the crunch as the knife slices through it. Hold it to your nose and smell that delightful fragrance. Look at the pulp and the triangular sections in the middle. Squeeze some juice out of it and feel it squirt on your face. Take a small bite and taste its tartness.

This easy exercise demonstrates the potency and "real-ness" of imagination. It stimulates nerve cells in our hands, face, ears, eyes, nose and mouth. And of course, it excites our taste buds and produces salivation. So imagination may begin as simple mental activity, but it quickly becomes a dynamic reality. It not only focuses our perceptions and expands our awareness; imagination creates very real experiences. But the best news is that imagination is a very potent and extremely pleasurable path to OBS.

Return to the Garden of Eden

The following exercise uses imagination to create a sensuous rendezvous at a heavenly waterfall of love. You may plan to share the exercise with a lover. It's OK if you do not currently know a special lover. Your unique love-mate is in the stream of universal consciousness searching for you at this very moment. Soon you will bathe together in the essence of love.

>Just listen to your tape, allow yourself to relax and accept your experiences. Your perceptions may be different from anything that you have ever perceived before. Afterwards you may have difficulty describing your experience in words. Avoid attempts to analyze, monitor or categorize. Just let go and feel the pleasure expand into ever-increasing waves of ecstasy.

>Begin by preparing yourself and your room, the space within and the space all around you. Allow your preparations to be slow and leisurely. Savor your own personal relaxation ritual. You are preparing for a journey back to the garden of paradise. And you joyfully anticipate your walk in this heavenly garden that you know so well.

>Soon you will bathe in a pool of warm, penetrating love — love which will nourish the seeds of intimacy that live within you. You know that you have always carried the seeds of these exotic flowers deep inside of yourself. And you have waited and yearned for their rebirth.

>When you are relaxed, quiet and centered, begin to travel in your mind's eye, in your imagination, to the beach. Visualize yourself lying on the beach on your beach

towel with that soft, warm sand beneath you. It's a beautiful spring day, not too warm nor too cool, but just warm enough to keep you perfectly comfortable. Just enjoy watching one or two fluffy clouds drifting against that clear blue sky.

There's no place that you need go and nothing that you need do. You have all the time in the world, because you are entering a place where time will cease to exist. And you will become lost in waves of ecstasy like you have never felt before.

It feels so good lying on the beach, watching the clouds drift by and listening to the sound of the waves. You find peace in the sound of waves as mother ocean plays that song that has been played for men and women for centuries and centuries. The music of the waves washes away all the cares of your day — all the cares of your lifetime. Your mind becomes calm and blank. You feel a new inner harmony with an inexplicable kind of tranquility.

You enjoy running your fingers through that loose, warm sand and feeling the cool water splash playfully against your toes. You look upward and watch the seagulls as they drift and float against that clear blue sky. As you watch the seagulls, you know that you too can drift and float. You can fly freely out of your body.

You are so very relaxed — deeply, completely relaxed. And you are now entering that mode of awareness which allows you to travel beyond the ordinary. Your spiritual mind is becoming open and receptive — receptive to new perceptions and wondrous new experiences. A strange kind of togetherness washes over you. It occurs to you that you are not alone. You have never been alone, even though you have often felt scared and lonely.

You begin to walk along the beach with one foot in that loose, dry, warm sand and the other foot in that wet, hard-packed, cool sand. And you listen to the sound of the waves, watch the seagulls, feel the warmth of sun and the coolness of that gentle breeze. As you walk along the beach, you notice the sensuous stirring of anticipation deep inside yourself. In the deepest inner core of your being, the seeds of intimacy are sprouting. Soon you will meet the love-mate for which you have always yearned.

You walk along the beach until you see a path leading away from the beach — a flirtatious, little path that beckons you to choose. You follow the path and discover that it meanders beside a beautiful, sparkling little stream. This is the stream of expanded consciousness which leads you to the garden of paradise.

How you cherish the garden of paradise with its heavenly waterfall of love! Here, you can experience an indescribable merging of souls. You are so happy to be walking along the path beside the stream of expanded consciousness. It feels so good to be back in the paradise that you know and love.

Now you are entering a magical rain forest. And there's a gentle mist caressing your face. It feels wonderful and sends tingling chills of pleasure all over your body. Feel this cool, gentle mist caressing your face and spreading down into your arms and chest. Just let go and relax into the pleasure.

Suddenly, you see a rainbow, a rainbow that shines across the path and offers a guiding light. It's such a beautiful rainbow — a rainbow that presents a kaleidoscope of colors — swirling around you as it guides you along the pathway. You feel somewhat like a child, a child following the rainbow.

You are feeling extraordinarily in touch, highly attuned and incredibly sensitive. It's as though you can see, hear, sense and know things more clearly than ever before. Your perception has expanded beyond the ordinary. You can see beyond the trees, ascending upward with your vision. You are becoming acutely aware of everything in all directions. You are now especially aware of your divine love-mate, who is journeying to the waterfall from a different direction along a path similar, but different from yours.

The magic of the rainbow seems to expand your perception. So you can now ascend upward beyond the trees and see the big picture while you are experiencing all the smallest details. You can see the great love of your life strolling along an individual pathway — a unique, delightful path leading to the waterfall of love. Already, you are feeling the love energy radiating to you. It's as though you walk intertwined together with your mate, even though you walk on separate paths.

Just continue to follow the rainbow — that kaleidoscope of colors. As you hear the music of cascading water, you begin to flow into the ecstasy of limitless intimacy. When you approach the waterfall, old feelings of loneliness become a myth of the past. You feel a sense of connectedness — connectedness with all of life. Outdated ideas of time and space are now irrelevant. And you know there is no limit to how good you can feel.

When you arrive at the waterfall of love, you are entranced by the exquisite beauty, more beauty than you have ever imagined. Qualities in the rainbow are now merging with qualities in the waterfall. You are perceiving with all the five senses simultaneously. And there is more, beyond the five senses, beyond the four dimensions. There is so much more.

Your love-mate has arrived with you and you feel and perceive simultaneously, as though you are one. Communication is automatic and perfect. The beauty of your mate is indescribable. It is beauty beyond the physical, beyond what we ordinarily perceive. Your mate is the essence of everything that you have ever labeled beautiful. And you are a mirror reflection of that incomparable beauty.

Radiant light energy gently leads you into that wonderful little pool. The rainbow has become part of the cascading waterfall. And all around you are liquid diamonds of beauty — billions of iridescent droplets of love. At long last you bathe in the essence of love.

There is a thunderfall of light and love all around you. You can see all beautiful colors in this light, hear all melodic sounds and feel all sensuous textures. Birds are singing a unique symphony which intermingles with the joyous music of the waterfall. And there is a wonderful smell in the air — like gardenias and roses and exotic perfume — floating on the breeze. You can taste the sweetness in the air, like cotton candy crystallizing on your tongue.

You are one with your mate, bathing together in that warm, penetrating pool of love. And there is that feeling you get just before orgasm — an electric elation of every fiber in your being. The seeds of intimacy have blossomed forth into magnificent flowers which encircle you and float all around the pool of love. There is a complete merging of souls as you embrace the very essence of life itself. You are completely immersed within the experience. You are the experience and it is alive like you are alive. You are here now — heavenly love, total intimacy and indescribable ecstasy are shared with your mate. And you can share the rapture again and again — forever.

When you are ready to refocus your awareness, simply count out loud, counting slowly from one to ten. Allow yourself to become more alert and awake with each count.

We have discovered abundant pathways to ecstasy. And the intimacy for which we yearn is only a step away. We have developed our skills for fixating and moving our awareness. We are learning how to experience through imaging and how to transfer our consciousness while imaging. So it is easy for us to let our imaginations become very real experiences. When we free our creativity, we can enjoy new and delightful love-making adventures.

Mental Sex

In the past, we have limited our love-making and falsely believed that we could not make love with our minds. But of course, we can make love with our minds. Actually good love-making takes place in our minds, not in our genitals. Our genitals are simply points of fixation for us. Tantric yoga presents wonderful exercises which enhance mental love-making to create a very intense sexual union. So tantric yoga can be another effective pathway to OBS. Let's remember that the best love-making is intensely spiritual and divinely sexual.

Out-of-body sex is real. It is a repeatable phenomenon, but difficult to explain when using a typical left-brain approach. OBS is a state of higher consciousness, an expanded form of perception. Although OBS is a very mental experience, it stimulates significant physical events, such as chemical changes in the brain and bloodstream which can be observed or measured. OBS is a highly mental, physically linked, intensely spiritual, sexual experience.

The depth, scope and passion of OBS are infinite. OBS can hover eternally outside of time, or transcend aeons in a split second. Any attempt to analyze OBS usually only serves to restrict the experience. And the most important knowledge of OBS is obtained by experience. Remember that it is impossible to tell someone what it feels like to have an orgasm. So it is with OBS — our words are always shallow attempts to explain an ecstasy that is so far beyond words.

Once we have experienced the ecstasy, explanations become superfluous. When we truly know, we know that we know. All of us can experience this indescribable rapture again and again. Our skill levels automatically improve each and every time we practice a few simple, pleasurable exercises. When we relax and invite OBS, it becomes a cherished guest who seduces us into the bliss of limitless intimacy.

Affirmations

Affirmations are a wonderful way to improve our self-confidence and reinforce the information we are learning. Affirmations which are individually designed are extremely effective. If you have never created your own affirmations, you may be surprised to discover how easy it is. Just avoid negatives and make your affirmations very positive. To help you get started we have presented some partial statements, so that you can just complete the sentences.

1. ....abundant pathways to ecstasy.

2. ....the wonder and glory of OBS.

3. ....the divinely spiritual sexuality within me.

4. ....increasing my perceptions and expanding my awareness.

5. ....projecting my awareness to invite OBS.

6. I rejoice in my ever-increasing skills for ....

7. All my pathways lead me to ....

8. My own spiritual love-mate ....

9. I can fly free easily and get high naturally simply by............

10. I am a beautiful, wonderful ....

Selected Readings

Bandler, Richard and Grindler, John. *The Structure of Magic*, Science and Behavior Books, Palo Alto, California, 1975.

Bandler, Richard and Grindler, John. *Frogs Into Princes: Neurolinguistic Programming*, Real People Press, Moab, Utah, 1979.

Bristol, Claude M. *The Magic of Believing*, Simon and Schuster, New York, 1969.

Dossey, Larry. *Recovering the Soul: A Scientific and Spiritual Search*, Bantam Books, New York, 1989.

Garrison, Omar. *Tantra: The Yoga of Sex*, Julian Press, New York, 1964.

Gawain, Shakti. *Creative Visualization*, Bantam Books, Inc., New York, 1982.

Houston, Jean. *The Possible Human: A Course in Enhancing Your Physical, Mental and Creative Abilities*, J. P. Tarcher, Inc., Los Angeles, California, 1982.

LaBerge, Stephen. *Lucid Dreaming*, Ballantine Books, New York, 1985.

Maltz, Maxwell. *The Magic Power of Self Image Psychology*, Prentice Hall, Englewood Cliffs, New Jersey, 1964.

Peale, Norman Vincent. *Positive Imaging: The Powerful Way to Change Your Life*, Ballantine Books, New York, 1982.

Rogo, Scott. *Leaving the Body*, Prentice Hall, New York, 1983.

Williams, Paul. *Das Energi*, Warner Books, New York, 1973

6

ANTICIPATING THE SEDUCTION

The Joy of Anticipation

A divine process of transformation is occurring — we are all ascending into a higher state of consciousness that allows us to fully affirm our spiritual sexuality. When we open ourselves to the beauty and love that surround us, we can easily rise above the limitations of SAWNKI. To feel the ecstasy and embrace limitless intimacy, we need only allow ourselves to anticipate the natural process of spiritual seduction.

Anticipating seduction allows us to enter a delightful altered state of consciousness. This thrilling ASC is often accompanied by a sweet taste in the back of our throats, butterflies in our stomachs and pupils expanding with excitement. When we anticipate spiritual union, we look forward to abundant love, divine goodness and endless pleasure. We also have an eager but calm assurance that whatever is about to happen will be life affirming. When we are in this state of positive receptivity, anyone can look at us and tell that we are "high."

This "high" feeling or positive anticipation blesses us with an enormous, peaceful power and energy. Healthy, happy children are often "high" and have abundant energy. If we observe a happy little child, we will see joyful anticipation. Let's remember that it is never too late to have a happy childhood. We can all be reborn into a happy child again and again.

An Invitation to Beauty and Pleasure

When we anticipate joyful, yet unknown events and believe in the gifts of ecstasy and intimacy, then we can embrace the out-of-body sexual experience. This heavenly spiritual seduction is an invitation to unite with beauty and pleasure. We can give a tantalizing invitation or receive one, but seduction just happens; we do not make it happen. We can anticipate and wait for the ecstasy, but it comes when we let go of worry and just feel beautiful — when we accept and know that we are all truly beautiful.

Seduction is an invitation to pleasure and beauty and freedom. It begins with our perception of and attraction to beauty. Our perceptions of beauty awaken our spiritual/sexual energy and thrill us with an eager aliveness. Beauty is a vibrant, living force that has profound positive effects on our minds, bodies and spirits. Each time we perceive beauty, we create pleasure. And the more beauty we perceive, the more pleasure we feel.

Nature, the great artist, provides us with abundant beauty. And it is the best kind of beauty because it is forever changing, from morning to night, summer to winter and moment to moment. What beauty have you flirted with today? Have you touched a flower to your lips? Winked at a sunset? Caressed a tree? Rejoiced with a bird's song? Or perhaps made love with the ocean?

We are blessed with so many places to experience beauty, so many ways to perceive beauty. Beauty is all around us — in people, in nature and in things. As we continue to free ourselves from negative beliefs, we can identify more closely with beauty and then everything becomes even more beautiful. To see beauty, it is important to think beautiful thoughts and speak beautiful words. Let's look at everything with the idea of finding something new and wonderful and beautiful. Soon we will discover that all beauty comes from within and is an inseparable part of each of us.

Reflections of Our Beauty

When we perceive something as beautiful, we are really seeing the beauty within us and it feels so good. For example, when we gaze at the stars we are reminded of our link to infinity and freedom. The beauty of the night sky seduces us into an expanded awareness of all that we are. The heavens invite us, as we unconsciously invite them, to a natural and pleasurable embrace.

To experience the ecstasy of spiritual seduction, it is important for us to perceive beauty and feel beautiful. Nothing outside of ourselves can be truly beautiful unless we first feel it within. Too often, we are disenchanted with our physical appearances. So we tend to focus on our imaginary flaws or criticize ourselves for what we think we lack. But let's remember that we are all beautiful in our divine spiritual forms.

Take a moment to close your eyes and imagine that you have a large crystal bowl full of dynamic, sparkling liquid light. Design your own personal ethereal self with this vibrant light. Arrange and re-arrange the light until you succeed in perceiving yourself as the true essence of beauty. Doesn't it feel wonderful to see yourself as perfect beauty? Can you imagine how attractive you are to your starmate at this very moment?

Of course, the attraction between ethereal beings is intense. It is so intense, so wonderful that it defies explanation. And words are always inadequate, shallow attempts to describe the essence of beauty in our starmates. It is only by experiencing this heavenly beauty and attraction that we begin to understand it.

An Effortless Seduction

Ultimately it is the experience which seduces us; we don't really seduce each other. The ideal seduction is free-flowing and effortless. It just happens. There is an absence of monitoring and evaluating. Instead there is a great deal of freedom and permission, beauty and pleasure. The experience simply overwhelms the rational processes. This is the letting go and it is so, so wonderful.

Here is a description of a spiritual seduction as told by a spiritual teacher who was unexpectedly, but very strongly drawn into a student's experience. This is how out-of-body sex begins. Note the combination of peacefulness and intensity, freedom and pleasure in this experience. Also note that leaving the body was easy, automatic and effortless; the experience itself just naturally invited the seduction.

> *It's really been a rather unique day for me in many ways and the effects of it seem to be lingering with me. It's almost dark and very peaceful now, and strangely, quietly still. And I wanted to take a few minutes to see if I could somehow put into words the things that I experienced earlier today with you, experiences that seem to be so far beyond explanation. And I think it's really because they are beyond rationality, beyond what we are accustomed to thinking and speaking of, that we really don't have words to explain them.*
>
> *But I want to try. I think it's important that I try and that I try to understand. And I genuinely want to share the experience with you, although I realize that I already have shared it with you and that words are superfluous at this point. But if we're going to communicate to others, then I do want to try to put it into the words no matter how inaccurate, how incomplete they may be.*
>
> *Today when you and I were working together, I knew that your experience was a much more successful experience and*

I could feel it. I could feel your presence in the room. And the strangest thing happened. I could feel myself easily, naturally, automatically, non-trying, effortlessly wanting to leave and not only wanting to, but actually leaving my body. I could feel the process happening, because of your presence in the room. Particularly, I could feel you behind and around me, and . . . so difficult to explain it.

But I could feel that presence and I could feel the possibilities. I knew what the next steps were going to be. It was an automatic thing that I was leaving my body, very naturally, with no apprehension, with no fear, with no restraint, just a kind of flowing thing that was occuring.

I was obviously losing the role as leader. I began to have trouble talking and the rational processes began to shut down. I felt the sensation of energy. I could see the light in the room, the translucent presence that I recognized as you and myself too — my spirit leaving and going, rising out of my body and that translucent awareness that was there. I began to feel this tremendous kind of pleasure that was combined with peacefulness somehow, an intensity that was free from anxiety, an intensity free from guilt, an intensity free from fear, an energized potency of light and color and pleasure and . . . .

What kept me from sort of completing the transition was my role as leader. I was drifting in and out, never completely allowing myself to leave my body, but I kept being seduced into leaving my body. It's not as though you in particular were seducing me, but the experience was seducing me. And what was so wonderful is that it was a kind of feeling of seduction that I've never experienced before, because it was the ideal seduction situation. It was seduction without pressure, seduction with a great deal of permission, seduction with a great deal of freedom. There was the absence of expectation and the absence of monitoring — a very free-flowing happening. So it was very different from any ration-

al or experiential understanding that I have of seduction. There's no doubt that it had a very intense sexual component to it, but not sex as I now know it. It definitely was very sensual, very sexual.

There was the beginning of a kind of osmosis with you. Even though I hadn't made the transition, I could feel an osmosis of energy and a tremendous kind of pleasurable experience that went with it. And when you combine that with freedom, I knew what the experience was like, what it is that we are all seeking. Somehow, I have a new awareness of it now, a new understanding.

I'm not sure that I can put it into words. It was a tremendous desire to suspend the rational processes, to become enmeshed in feeling and flowing emotion, to become enmeshed in perceptual, instinctual processes. It was like a sensation of almost returning to infancy. And it was certainly a beginning to move beyond rationality, beyond the limits of the body.

We wish you could hear the tone of voice of this person, the inflections, pauses and emotions. They communicate far more than the written words. The rapture and awe in this individual's voice not only convince us of the reality of the experience, but also help us understand the incomparable ecstasy of spiritual seduction. But the best news is that we all have abundant opportunities to enjoy this heavenly seduction. And when we experience it ourselves, then we truly understand.

In this seduction, the leader had no expectation of being drawn into the student's experience, since it opposed the role as guide. However the teacher and student had been working together for a few months on past-life regression and were spiritually linked. The student had practiced meditation and entered an altered state of consciousness easily. During this session the student wanted to investigate a time and place where OBEs were common. The session began with imagery of lying in a hammock. Afterwards the student was asked to describe the experience while still deeply relaxed.

> *I noticed that when I'm regressed, it goes in steps. There are perceptual jumps. For example, when I'm in the hammock, suddenly I realize I'm not there anymore. Not only is there a jump from this chair to the hammock, but there's another jump to another place. I keep jumping like that, and can go a long way very quickly. All I have to do is say, "I'm not here anymore." Each time I seek a different place, I say, "I'm not here anymore," and it takes a split second. It's so easy, almost effortless.*
>
> *There were elements of ecstasy in the experience. We were all flying in the night sky, yet the landscape was brightly lit. We could see in the dark. I thought it was wonderful, yet I got the impression from the other people that it was no big deal, just another activity to them.*
>
> *I became aware of you beginning to join me later when my experience jumped to a higher level. I was drawn into the sun and experiencing the connectedness of all suns, all stars. At that time, I felt you beginning to come up into that beautiful mystical condition I was in. It felt unusual or strange to be connected to you in that way, as if I were in two places at the same time. I felt that you were asking permission to join me. I had no expectations, just a very permissive feeling of trust. The experience was very free-flowing and wonderful.*

Note that the student trusted himself and the leader implicitly, giving total permission, letting go of expectation, limits and fears. Perhaps more to the point, he gave permission for the experience to unfold as it would. Notice his "jumps." He does not choose a specific destination; he just goes. Here we see the elements of complete freedom.

Let's look at these two experiences to understand more about seduction and OBS. Obviously, there is a strong element of pleasure in the experiences. The student looked forward to a pleasurable experience and considered the sessions playful explorations. A meditative, relaxed, clear state was an important part of the experience. Perhaps this was mostly a state of open permissiveness which tends to invite OBS. Note that the student does not seem to be fully aware of the exact process, but it works very well anyway. So we see elements of anticipation, pleasure, invitation, permission, relaxation and play. These are common characteristics of seduction.

A Tantalizing Love Exercise

The following exercise is designed to create a tantalizing feeling of sexual anticipation. You may invite your mate, lover or a friend to share this exercise with you. If you continue the exercise for about five minutes (which may seem like hours), it is quite possible to reach orgasm. After reading over the exercise, you may wish to record it and play it back during the exercise. Avoid talking during the exercise, but speak to your partner with your eyes and your feelings.

> Sit facing each other in a comfortable position, close together. Place your left hand over your partner's heart, letting it extend slightly over her left breast. Allow your partner to place her left hand over your heart. Now place your right hand on top of her left which is positioned over your heart. Let your partner place her right hand on top of your left which is positioned over her heart.
>
> Now stare deeply, directly into the eyes — those beautiful eyes that are true windows to the soul. Continue to become lost in the eyes, those wonderful eyes through which all love is automatically communicated. Become lost in the eyes which sparkle with energy and glisten with emotion. Become aware of your heartbeat and your partner's heartbeat. Feel the breathing, breathing each free and gentle and easy breath together. You are now

sharing the very essence of life with each breath that you take, breathing in the same air.

You are exchanging energy in the very air that you breathe. The air which has been inside your partner is now inside of you. You can feel your heart beating. You can feel your partner's heart beating. It is so beautiful breathing together, hearts beating together, feeling the essence of life together. You are loving your partner with pure positive thought energy, touching and stroking your partner mentally. The eyes feel, receive and give abundant love energy. You can feel it flowing in waves all over your body, from your toes up your body into your partner and returning — ebb and flow, back and forth, in and out — sharing more and more, feeling the love energy.

You are becoming a channel of flowing energy. You can feel the tingling energy flowing from your body to your partner's body and back again. The connection between your hands and arms and bodies provides a circuit for the flow of spiritual, sexual energy. Tingling energy is flowing through your body to your partner, from your partner back into you. It's such a beautiful feeling — hearts beating together as one — every life's breath breathed as one. The eyes give perfect communications of love, touching and stroking mentally with the eyes.

You are becoming lost in the experience now — just perceiving and flowing, flowing waves of energy from one body to the other. The longer you look into those beautiful eyes, the more and more aroused you become. You can feel that glowing, eager sexual arousal, that indescribable kind of anticipation. And you may notice an unusual peacefulness along with your arousal. But there's a quickening of the spirit and a tingling of the genitals. Just allow yourself to become lost in the free-flowing intensity of the experience. Let the intimacy build until it takes you to new heights of ecstasy and new levels of love.

How does it feel to communicate intimately without words? For many of us, it is a new and different type of sharing. Once we become comfortable with this type of sharing, it is so delightful to communicate without words. Words can be wonderful also, but too often we use words in negative ways because we are afraid. Then words can hide the depths of our passions and block intimacy. With practice, we can increase our positive non-verbal communication skills and give ourselves and others permission to feel and perceive more deeply.

Non-Verbal Links to OBS

If you regularly spend time with a special friend or lover, you have an excellent opportunity for practicing non-verbal communication. Simply increase the amount of quiet relaxation time you spend together and practice speaking lovingly with your eyes and your thoughts. Or touch your lover without touching, mentally running your hands over your lover's body. As you increase loving, non-verbal communication, you will automatically receive delicious invitations for OBS.

One way to develop non-verbal communication skills is simply to sit across from your partner, perhaps touching casually and gazing into each other's eyes. Become aware of the totality of your sensations, rather than concentrating on one perception. An integrated, holistic awareness leads to OBS. So experience your partner's breathing, see your reflection in his eyes, feel the texture of her clothes or skin, smell her hair, become aware of the warmth of his body. Do all these things simultaneously. Experience the whole and all its facets in one eternal moment.

You may begin to see a light surrounding the outline of your partner's body. Allow this light to radiate fully and then ask yourself "What are the colors of arousal?" How would the color of this aura or halo of light change as your partner becomes aroused? What, for example, would be the color of orgasm? If you have difficulty seeing auras, darken the room and place a soft light behind your partner and another behind yourself. Observe the changing light rays and become lost in the beauty of the radiating colors. Identify with the colors and feel the beauty and pleasure inside of you. Let the experience unfold freely, giving yourself permission to combine SAWNKI with these new and delightful love-making experiences.

Let's remember that the kind of communication which occurs during OBS is non-verbal, non-abstract, non-symbolic. It is direct and perfect. In the OBS state, words are superfluous. This is good reason to turn off the verbal or left side of the brain as a prelude to OBS. We can easily shift to the right brain by providing it with the kinds of stimuli it likes to process. We want to emphasize positive emotional and sensory images. When we share smiles, laughter, play, touching, hugs and joyful togetherness, we are automatically stimulating the right brain and inviting OBS. Relaxation, visualization, imagination and dreaming also provide delightful pathways for activating the right brain. In addition, we can observe and create multiple sensory images of great pleasure. We have already discovered that beautiful outdoor settings naturally awaken all our senses, but indoor settings can also be created which are equally engaging.

Creating A Love Ritual

Perhaps at the beginning of our desire to have these wonderfully pleasurable experiences, we need a plan. We have abundant opportunities to create conditions which will invite OBS. We can create romantic, sensuous environments which excite us and expand our emotional perceptions. A married couple we know sets aside one weekend each month and secludes themselves in their bedroom. They joyfully anticipate ecstasy and intimacy with special treats of food, wine, bubble bath, candles, massage oil, flowers and so forth. Another couple goes to a different hotel each month for a weekend of passionate play and adventure.

It is helpful to create a delightful ritual when we understand its true purpose, which is to open our creative minds. Then we can suspend rational thinking for awhile and become lost in the ecstasy of perceiving, flowing and feeling. Emphasizing sensual experiences helps to shift awareness over to the right side of the brain where OBS begins. Thus, anything which stimulates the senses in a pleasant, peaceful or sensuous way can be used to set the mood. This includes music, flowing water, incense or perfume, erotic pictures, candles or special lighting, soft rugs and sensuous clothing. Simply choose whatever pleases you, as long as the end result is a quiet and sensuous mind free of distracting thoughts. Ultimately we find that we never needed these things, but they helped us to focus our awareness toward something sensuous which was always there.

If you currently have a mate or lover with whom you regularly enjoy SAWNKI, then you may want to expand your lovemaking to create a more intimate spiritual experience. Intimacy and spiritual bonding occur most easily when we share our sensuous feelings in a quiet and leisurely manner. So you may want to include a leisurely period of positive, non-verbal communication and gentle touching in your sensuous rituals.

If you share intercourse or oral sex, allow yourself to mentally travel inside of your partner's body and feel the pleasure which he is feeling from the inside out. Then travel inside of your own body and become aware of millions of pleasure receptors — twinkling and sparkling with ever-increasing ecstasy. Become totally lost in the pleasure inside of your own body. Feel the electric elation of each cell continue to build until you are swept into that incredible explosion of orgasmic fusion. This simple method of mental traveling is a very effective technique for expanding SAWNKI into a more dynamic spiritual/physical union.

An Energy Triangle

Here is a another simple technique which will help invite OBS. It may be enjoyed with or without a partner. Place two pillows on the floor about ten feet apart. Sit on one pillow and have your partner sit on the other facing you. If you do not have a partner, fixate your gaze in the direction of the other pillow and invite your starmate to join you. Visualize or imagine a silver thread running along the floor under the pillows and up to the ceiling to form a triangle. If you have difficulty visualizing, you may actually place a ribbon along the floor under the pillows running it up to the ceiling and taping it to form a triangle.

Relax, become centered and focused on love. Repeat the love mantra and communicate non-verbally, touching and stroking with your thoughts. Soon you will begin to feel the exchange of love energy flowing from your feet along the path of the ribbon to your partner. Allow this beautiful love energy to flow and commingle, stroking and touching gently, almost imperceptibly at first. This vibrant energy will continue to build so that it forms a dynamic circuit and becomes more than the two of you. Experience the positive energy force pushing you up the ribbon to the apex of the triangle. Relax and go with the flow. Soon you will see and feel your ethereal self floating near the ceiling. Contact the translucent presence of your partner and begin to embrace her with your astral body. The natural process of spiritual seduction will now occur automatically and effortlessly. Just continue to relax and anticipate the ecstasy. Soon you will become dancing laser beams, harmonizing and blending in endless orgasmic fusion.

Free and Easy Choices

Which exercises presented in this book are the most pleasurable for you? Exercises, rituals, meditations and so forth are openings which allow us to focus and expand our awareness. Sometimes they are like windows which help us to perceive more clearly and feel a fresh, warm aliveness. Pleasurable activities tend to be the most life affirming. We have presented many different techniques throughout the book to allow for free and easy selection. If one exercise doesn't appeal to you, simply choose another. Practice the exercises you enjoy and you will successfully expand your awareness and embrace limitless intimacy. Feel free to design your own exercises, just make sure that they are very positive. It is OK if you do not currently have a mate or lover. Each of us has a special starmate with whom we can unite spiritually and sexually. So choose your favorite exercises, invite your starmate to meet you and expand your awareness to embrace the ecstasy.

There are so many effective ways to induce heavenly out-of body experiences. For example, you may discover that you can relax each part of your body and just tell your spiritual mind to leave your body as you exhale slowly. Or you may simply concentrate on your forehead and allow your consciousness to flow out the top of your head. To travel to a friend or lover's home, ask permission to visit, then tell yourself that you are going there and relax deeply. While you are relaxing, visualize that special person and tell yourself to leave your body. With practice, OBE really can be this easy! If you are having minimal results, just remain positive and have fun practicing. OBE and OBS are learned skills and different individuals will be successful with different techniques. So just choose your favorite techniques, keep practicing and you will be successful.

If you have been doing the exercises in this book and are having difficulty experiencing yourself as spirit, you may want to consult a professional hypnotist who is open to helping you explore past lives. Let's remember that spirituality and sexuality are innately intertwined and inseparable. So sexual problems may mask unresolved spiritual issues or religion may be used to hide sexual problems. We have found it beneficial to ask a hypnotist to help us regress to a lifetime where we were fully integrated sexually and spiritually. Past life regression can affirm our sexuality and help resolve karmic problems. It can provide a demonstration of spiritual existence and personal immortality. And past life regression may also facilitate the natural process of spiritual seduction.

Spiritual seduction is the perfect, heavenly seduction because it is effortless, yet has an incomparable intensity of pleasure combined with total freedom and permission. It begins with our awareness of divine beauty, beauty which entrances and invites us. Then there is a tremendous anticipation of the ecstasy which we sense to be a part of the experience. And there is the beginning of a new kind of intimacy — a limitless intimacy where communication is perfect and automatic. It is a freer seduction — free from typical worries about looks, performance, disease, pregnancy and other restrictions. Let's consider the possibilities. OBE and OBS are keys to limitless intimacy, total freedom and ecstasy beyond compare. If someone were to offer us a magic key which would open the door to the castle of our dreams, would we accept it?

Affirmations

Affirmations help us to anticipate positive outcomes. When we affirm with enthusiasm, we have taken the first positive step towards the creation of a cherished event. Affirmations which are individually designed are extremely effective. We have presented some partial statements to help you become accustomed to creating your own personal affirmations. Simply complete the sentences with words that feel good to you.

1. . . . . anticipate the natural process of spiritual seduction.

2. . . . . accept the gifts of abundant love, divine goodness and endless pleasure.

3. . . . . am really seeing the beauty within me.

4. . . . . to fully affirm my glorious spiritual sexuality.

5. . . . . so that I can communicate more intimately and feel more deeply.

6. Whenever I see beauty in the world . . . .

7. OBS is my magic key to . . . .

8. I can have limitless intimacy, total freedom and ecstasy beyond compare when . . . .

9. I rejoice in my abundant opportunities for . . . .

10. To feel ecstasy and embrace limitless intimacy, I need only . . . .

Selected Readings

Barbach, Lonnie and Levine, Linda. *Shared Intimacies,* Doubleday, Garden City, New York, 1980.

Dass, Ram. *Journey of Awakening: A Meditator's Guidebook,* Bantam Books, New York, 1978.

Fiore, Edith. *You Have Been Here Before*, Ballantine Books, New York, 1978.

Garfield, Patricia. *Pathway to Ecstasy*, Holt, Rhinehart and Winston, New York, 1979.

Garrison, Omar V. *Tantra: the Yoga of Sex*, Julian Press, New York, 1964.

McCuen, William G. *The Bicameral Brain and Human Behavior*, Vantage Publishing, New York, 1986.

Ramsdale, David and Dorfman, Ellen. *Sexual Energy Ecstasy*, Peak Skill Publishing, Playa Del Rey, California, 1985.

Stanway, Andrew. *The Art of Sensual Loving: A New Approach to Sexual Relationships*, Carroll and Graf Publishers, New York, 1989.

Sturgeon, Theodore. *Godbody*, New American Library, New York, 1987.

Sutphen, Dick. *Predestined Love: Authentic Case Histories of Reincarnation*, Pocket Books, New York, 1988.

Thornton, L., Sturtevant, J., and Sumerall, A., Editors. *Touching Fire: Erotic Writings By Woman*, Carroll and Graf Publishers, New York, 1989.

Yorke, Andrew. *The Art of Erotic Massage*, Javelin Books, New York, 1989.

7

THE ECSTASY OF SPIRITUAL BONDING

Our Spiritual Flight

SAWNKI (Sex As We Now Know It) can be great, but we often feel a vague dissatisfaction or sense something missing. We long to form a more intimate bond with another and to share an intense, lingering ecstasy. At the same time, we strive for freedom and individuality. We want it all but we have assumed that we cannot have it all. The glorious truth is that we can have it all right now if we choose. For within each of us, within the creative consciousness of our minds, we have boundless opportunities for love, ecstasy, intimacy, freedom and complete fulfillment. All of these gifts are our spiritual birthrights which we are now ready to accept.

We are divine spirits who have travelled a difficult road discovering this greatest of all truths about ourselves. Sometimes we have limited our growth and restricted our pleasure, because we failed to recognize how beautiful and wonderful we really are. But a miraculous transformation is finally occurring. We are now in the process of inviting communion with our own souls. And as we open the doors of our consciousness, we can embrace the ecstasy of limitless intimacy.

Our consciousness is ready to take flight like a gorgeous butterfly emerging from its cocoon. While in the caterpillar stage, we have felt limited and imprisoned in some inexplicable way. But a marvelous change has been happening while we have been in our cocoons. Just below the surface, our consciousness has been growing and expanding to transform our lives and allow us to fully affirm our spiritual sexuality.

We are spiritual beings filled with divine sexual energy and are blessed with the gift of ever-expanding consciousness. We can freely and easily shift our awareness and create wonderful out-of-body experiences (OBEs). When we share out-of-body experiences, we can receive invitations to unite with our own special starmates and enjoy the rapture of out-of-body sex. OBS is heavenly spiritual sex which allows us to share the essence of love in the fullest sense.

A Sensuous Caress

Spiritual sex is really different from all other experiences. When we attempt to describe it, we often arrive at unusual or even contradictory word combinations, such as "non-invasive intimacy" or "calm and exciting." For example, here is what it feels like to be caressed sensuously by an out-of-body presence.

> *I awakened facing the clock — it was 3:15 a.m. I was aware of his presence in the room. Especially I was aware of the warmth of his presence and could recognize him by this warmth. It was a warmth that was uniquely his, different from anyone else's. Perhaps it was a warmth created by his energy. I don't know. I've never felt anything like it before. It's just so difficult to explain. I only know that it was a peaceful, but very erotic sense of warmth and I knew without question that it was him.*
>
> *I was lying on one side and when I awakened I was intensely aware of him touching me and the warmth of his touch. He*

was stroking my hair, shoulders and upper back. The sensation of warmth was so different — gentle, but very penetrating, like a vibrating warmth. It was like something that warms from inside every cell, but without heating you — so pleasurable but different — like the feeling you would get if you were chilled to the bone and then felt warm sun on your bare skin.

He kept stroking my hair very gently. And his touch was very loving and so sensuous. When he caressed my face, I felt vibrating waves of pleasure floating all over my body. At one point the ecstasy became so intense that I felt immobolized by the pulsating waves of pleasure. The experience lingered with me the next day. I just felt so happy and peaceful that I couldn't stop smiling.

Note the gentleness and intensity in this sexual experience, the soft penetration of touch, the peaceful arousal and exciting satisfaction. It seems so natural for these apparent contradictions to exist harmoniously. And there is an incredible ecstasy and lingering joy that has to be experienced to be understood. When we enjoy OBS like this, we are beginning to share in the deepest, most loving way.

Kaleidoscopes To OBS

Would you like to be blessed with this kind of sensuous intimacy? It really can be quite easy. Ask a close friend or lover for permission to visit them out-of-body. Then obtain a kaleidoscope. Let the child within you enjoy playing with the kaleidoscope. Hold it up to a light, turn it slowly, then rapidly and watch the swirling, changing patterns. Spend some leisurely time playing with this fascinating toy. Allow yourself to become lost in the colors that expand, contract and blend together to create everchanging patterns of beauty.

After several minutes, begin to visualize your lover's face in the center of the swirling colors and patterns. Allow your consciousness to enter the tunnel of the kaleidoscope. Tell yourself that you are going to visit this precious spirit. Feel yourself being drawn into the tunnel by the swirling, magical flower. With each tumbling click of the jewels, let yourself drift deeper and deeper into the colors surrounding your lover's face. Suddenly, in a twinkling jewel of a moment, you are there. Then the merging of souls occurs automatically, blessing you with a peaceful arousal and indescribable intimacy.

We sometimes invite this delicious intimacy by playing with the kaleidoscope before bedtime. As we drift into sleep, we visualize our lover's face in the beautiful, swirling flower. With this simple technique, it is so easy to awaken in a heavenly dream of rapture. Yes, OBS truly can be this easy!

OBS really begins with our affirmation of our spiritual sexuality. We have already discovered how easy it is to expand our consciousness and create exciting out-of-body experiences. And we know that spiritual seduction is a natural process which occurs when we open ourselves to the beauty and love that surround us. As we share OBS with another soul, we begin to form a spiritual bond which allows us to enjoy an indescribable ecstasy and embrace the bliss of limitless intimacy.

Spiritual Bonding

Have you ever felt lonely and yearned for deep intimacy and intense ecstasy? The rapture of spiritual bonding sweeps away the loneliness and yearning of SAWNKI. We reach this different and wonderful level of orgasm by re-entering the spiritual paradise from whence we came — a paradise that we were very close to as small children, and perhaps closest to in our mother's womb. Spiritual bonding is like the intimacy and peace that we have all experienced in the womb. But it is so much more because it includes aspects of freedom, separateness and ecstasy beyond compare.

Spiritual bonding is simply an expanded form of OBS which occurs when spiritual entities, who have freely and temporarily left their bodies, choose to unite souls. Their mutual orgasms produce an osmosis of energy that is simultaneously explosive and peaceful. It is like having an orgasm in every cell of your mind and body, and it is like nothing you have ever felt before. It may be accompanied by physical orgasm of the bodies. Imagine what it feels like to be kissed simultaneously all over your body — to dive into an ocean of sensation and float on timeless waves of pleasure, adrift on a sea of ecstasy. Doesn't this sound inviting?

A truly unforgetable experience, this vibrant blending of souls is very intense, yet it feels so soft, so gentle. Once we have shared it, life begins to develop an ecstatic glow that lingers with us for days, even weeks. Colors become brighter, sounds sweeter, people friendlier; challenges are easier, smiles omnipresent. The old myths of distance and separateness disappear and the emptiness inside is filled with peace and joy. The word "love" takes on new meanings and there is a natural movement toward harmony and balance. How wonderful it is to feel so alive, so loveable, so loved!

An Experience of Rapture

The following vignette has an ecstatic glow that is both exciting and peaceful. Note the joyous intensity and the complete merging of the two ethereal beings. This transcript is beautiful, but does not adequately express the rapture in the tone of voice. Suffice it to say that the speaker was very high from the experience and laughed a lot between words. She was at times overcome and unable to speak.

It was all beautiful. All of it was very beautiful. It was a rich, green, lush forest; fertile, with a lot of things growing and beautiful flowers. The river was liquid crystal. Rainbow light surrounded me in golds and reds and purples. My hair was glistening and glowing yellow.

And the waterfall was falling from heaven — it just came from nowhere, dropping thousands of tiny little crystals into a pool. The water in the pool was a deep, deep blue — almost so deep of a blue that it was literally just a pure color, more than a liquid.

And my mate wasn't really in human form, although he had a human shape. He was more spirit, rather than features of hair and teeth and all that. He was more color, pulsating deep blues and purples. It was just like he came to me and wrapped himself around me, where I was actually inside of him and he was inside of me. It was real pulsating.

At one point it was like we two came together, and merged, and then opened up into these flowers, and all the flowers burst forth with liquid crystals inside. It was real calming and yet exciting. My heart was racing, but I was also very calm. It made you want to stay, it made you want to be there forever. It was just wonderful. Why didn't we do this before?

Everything was color — it was purples on pinks, with all different shades — real vibrant colors, deep blacks and greens. They merged almost as a ball of energy that just kind of pulsated.

I seemed to be in human form. And he was almost like a shadow, sometimes less human, sometimes more human. It was like he shifted. I was in a human form until he came to me, then I became the color and shadow as we meshed together.

I was real golden, my hair glistening gold, my skin a darker gold; more than human — the perfect form of what a human can be. Once he came to me we were both translucent, bodies almost non-existent.

You could mesh together and neither would lose anything. At that point you became round with a center, like a bud opening up, inside filled with crystals — gorgeous, a lot of color. The colors were real intense, real vibrant. At times it was so intense, I would think, "Am I breathing? Do I need to breathe?"

It was just really beautiful, a lot of glittery, shiny. A part of me was just breathless, but yet a part of me was willing to be calm.

The level of spiritual bonding in this experience was quite intense. Note that the lovers were inside of each other, meshed together in a pulsating ball of energy. When asked what it would be like to share this experience with her lover during physical sex, the speaker was astonished and overwhelmed. We can all share this level of intensity when we open ourselves to the miracle of spiritual bonding.

Feeling Life As Children

We can compare the spiritual bonding as described above to the bond between mother and infant in the womb. This is an experience that we have all felt, and can feel again. It is an intimacy beyond compare, where even the same blood chemicals are shared. When a pregnant mother has sex, positive chemicals are released into her bloodstream and felt by the baby. When mother is happy, baby is happy. There is limitless love and intimacy between mother and baby. They are literally a part of each other. And this bond is very natural. Spiritual bonding is like a return to the natural intimacy of the womb, a return to a time when past and future, spirit and flesh, are one.

Do you recall a time in early childhood when you discovered something new? Perhaps you didn't know what it was, but you knew it was something BIG. Life was exciting. And that wonderful childhood naivete allowed you to experience abundant life — life that was free from limiting expectations. There was magic and you enjoyed an open, curious, very real exploration of your world. You were involved in direct experiences, not just talking about life, but moving into life. And sometimes life was moving into you, which was the most exciting of all.

As we grew up, we began to use symbols and models of reality more and more; we began to "think" and "speak" more. And although we still "feel" as adults, we often tend to subdue, repress or discount our feelings. It's as though we have learned to hang a veil of abstract labels between reality and ourselves. Sometimes we even believe that we know something simply because we can label it. But of course we can only "know" something by experiencing it.

A Journey Beyond Words

The following transcript is from a man who danced with his starmate and shared an experience that went far beyond words, even beyond thoughts. Note the special connectedness and mirroring movements of the starmates, the intuitive knowing and dynamic experiencing.

> *It was so wonderful. At first I was in and out, doing something like falling asleep, then drifting in and out of a dream state. I can't recall some of the specifics of how I left my body, like some processes were disconnected. I recall moving deeper into the relaxation and being aware that my mind was drifting. At first my body was heavier and then it shifted and became very light instead of heavy.*
>
> *I experienced a lot of color, especially moving toward the star and connecting with the star. There was a lot of swirl-*

ing colors and the colors were blended and intermingled. At some point of experiencing color, I began to become lost in the swirling color and was of it and was it, like I am the color.

I don't know exactly when I began to feel the shift in my body. It was somewhere around the point that you gave me permission to feel myself moving out of my body. I didn't exactly have a sense of being separated from my body. It was just that my body took on a different sensation, like I was still in body, but not in body. I didn't feel like a body.

The body, non-body that I experienced was . . . . I guess the best word to describe it is "expanded." It felt as if all the energy in my body was being pulled away from my body, but not disconnected just expanded. To the extent that I experienced a body, it felt as if my body, my arm for example, was out like this, expanded about a foot outward and all that expanded space was pure energy. I felt warm, tingling, not a physical tingling but just a sense of energy.

I'm continuing to be aware right now of feeling a lightness in my legs, my arms and my chest. It's not the sense of expandness that I felt while out of my body, but a similar sensation, more contracted, denser with a similar lightness and energy.

As I moved into the star, I was just feeling the energy, feeling the light flooding in. The star was a blue light and it became like — that's home for me. The light was not the shade of blue or the color intensity of blue that I would have expected it to be. It was much softer, a very pleasant, comfortable shade of blue. It was so easy to see the light and to feel myself filled with light. I was the light.

My starmate was an ideal woman although there were no particular features that I could attach to her. There wasn't a real sense of the physical with her. Her hair was more shadow, the darkness of light. The rest of her being was bathed in light. She was just beautiful, such beautiful white light, but without the limits of the physical.

We danced together, a kind of flying dancing. It was a mirroring movement of each other, flying together through the universe. There was a sense of connectedness, absolute connectedness as if all the chakras were connected with my starmate. It was a beautiful mirroring, moving together without need for communication.

The communication was remarkable. It was telepathic communication, yet no thoughts were exchanged, not thoughts as we know them. It was as if I were facing her and we were connected at all energy points, yet I was never aware of any thought transference. Telepathy is not really accurate, because there was never an exchange of thought. That's where the connectedness was so . . . . a oneness. Even the word "telepathy" is inaccurate. To me, telepathy implies unspoken communication and there's still thought words. But this experience was extraordinary, because it went beyond thoughts, beyond words, beyond mental telepathy.

There was this beautiful, intuitive knowing without words and a great sense of oneness. It was just a perfect mirroring and there was no sense of one or the other of us leading this wonderful dance. It was just being together, just flowing and flying with no sense of one leading and the other following. And there was no need to communicate about what to do. It was just doing together, being together . . . . so wonderful.

The ecstasy was very unusual, not passionate as I usually think of it. And it was not exactly a sense of peace, but an indescribable sense of being together. It's so difficult to describe it. There was a wonderful connection that went beyond judgement or non-judgement. It was even beyond a sensation or thought of being at peace. It was beyond thought. I don't have words to describe it. I keep looking for words, but there are none . . . . beyond words, beyond thought. It was pure experience, just being and the full experience of being.

I maintained a sense of physical separateness and individuality, but there was a oneness with the experience. So there was a sense of separateness and also connectedness through the chakras. At some point, I lost awareness of a separateness and was just experiencing. Then there was a sense of merging and just experiencing — a oneness. I don't know at what point I shifted.

The experience went beyond arousal, beyond peace and beyond ecstasy. It went beyond feeling as I have known it in the past, like existing in a state of peace and ecstasy, rather than feeling peace and ecstasy. It just "is" peace; it "is" ecstasy, not merely feeling peace and ecstasy. It goes beyond just feeling. It's more like I am peace; I am ecstasy. It is truly an "I am" experience; I am peace and ecstasy and goodness . . . . so wonderful.

As illustrated in the above transcript, our words are inadequate when we attempt to describe OBS. At some point in our spiritual expansion, we simply become the experience — we are peace, goodness and ecstasy. When this happens, we are like infants feeling deeply and embracing life fully without the words to describe or limit our experience.

Our Magnetic Life Force

What draws our souls together in this wonderful mating dance? We have all felt an intense attraction to someone special and it often feels as though there is a powerful magnetic force drawing us together. Perhaps we are drawn to each other for the sake of spiritual union. Just as atoms, molecules and cells are bonded together to create higher forms of life, so we are challenged to rise to a higher level of spiritual bonding. When our attractions radiate from our spiritual centers, we share the joy of unconditional love.

In spiritual/sexual bonding, there seems to be a resonance, a vibration of energy that draws our souls together. It's as though we have spiritual cells with permeable membranes through which love flows by the osmosis of sexual energy. This wonderful osmosis of love truly bonds us and frees us from the illusion of loneliness.

Our sexuality is our life force, our power source, the thread that links us with everything in the universe. If we deny or limit the spiritual aspect of sex, we may miss one of the most beautiful parts of life. Consider the moment of conception when spirit and body unite in the womb. Here is a direct link to all past and future generations, an affirmation of the unity of all people and a transcendence of time and death. We can feel all these miracles during sex, when we are open to the invitation provided by OBS. Our sexual union offers a very literal return to the womb, that heavenly gateway between paradise and paradise-on-Earth.

Affirming and Letting Go

To prepare ourselves for the ecstasy of spiritual bonding, we need only affirm our desire for OBS. Sometimes our routes to pleasure have not been life-giving. But spiritual sex is the most life-giving of all expressions. And we are created to be perfect expressions of abundant life. All we need do is just love the idea of OBS, for every atom in the universe responds joyously and creatively to love. So just love the idea of OBS and spiritual bonding, and you will soon feel the endless waves of rapture.

If we take a moment to honestly ask ourselves "what are our true expectations about spiritual bonding," then we can strip away limitations, or perhaps replace negative with positive beliefs. To be truly alive, we must be willing to walk naked into the unknown, trusting that life and the universe have only our best interests in mind. So our approach to spiritual sex is best made without any expectations at all, except the excited anticipation of a new and joyous experience. A complete openness to the experience can be encouraged if we are willing to forget what we know — forget what we know about ourselves, forget what we know about our partner, forget what we know about sex.

Sometimes our expectations shape or limit our experience in negative ways. An immigrant once asked William Penn what the people were like in Philadelphia. William Penn asked the newcomer what the people were like in his homeland. The stranger replied that they were ill-tempered and mean. To which Penn replied, "They are the same here." Later, another newcomer asked the same question. Penn again asked what the people were like in the homeland, and the immigrant replied that they were caring and kind. Of course, Penn replied, "They are the same here."

In spiritual bonding, we let go of expectations, forget about the outcome and allow ourselves to become enchanted with the process — just building arousal, relaxing and flowing. We simply become filled with love and concentrate on accepting and reflecting love. So spiritual seduction is a process which occurs naturally when we open ourselves to the love and beauty that surround us.

Although spiritual bonding is the height of ecstasy and intimacy, it is not something we can aim for; rather it is achieved by not trying, by letting go. For most of us, SAWNKI has been goal-oriented, "busy" sex. It's as though we have had an agenda and a limited amount of time to accomplish it. Often the goal has been releasing tension, achieving the orgasm and making sure our partner does the same. Let's remember that sex is never an urgency and we can savor it again and again.

Freedom and Goodness

In the spiritual realm where we fly during out-of-body sex, there exist only goodness and joy. There are no such things as sin or immorality. Concepts such as spiritual rape or out-of-body voyeurism are simply absurd. When out of the body, we can travel only where we are welcome. It is just not possible to cause harm or to be harmed. The very idea of harm is absent, and never was, never will be.

So while in this spiritual paradise, we are free from worries or doubts; everything just fits and the world is recognized as perfect and right after all. This freedom and goodness is why spiritual sex is so incredible. It is like the carefree play of young and innocent children who have the infinite power and goodness of the entire universe at their disposal.

We can all enter paradise-on-Earth when we affirm our spiritual sexuality. Our sexual energy is the life force which provides us with our power, vitality and zest for living. As we awaken this life force, we can share the ultimate intimacy through a merging of our souls. This rapturous spiritual bonding is the highest expression of love and provides us with the intimacy, ecstasy and freedom for which we yearn.

Seeds of Ecstasy

Each one of us experiences spiritual bonding in a unique, individual way. Just as each snowflake, fingerprint, sunrise and sunset is different, we too are unique and wonderful. So just choose the exercises which are most pleasurable for you, practice them and you will enjoy many glorious adventures with OBS. Doing the exercises in this book is like opening a fascinating series of Chinese boxes. Inside each exercise there are seeds which, if nurtured and cultivated, will burst forth into beautiful flowers of ecstasy and intimacy. And each shared exercise opens a more precious box full of ecstasy leading to the bliss of limitless intimacy.

Each of us has a starmate with whom we can share the rapture of spiritual bonding. The following exercise is designed to allow you to fly with your special starmate. Listen to a tape recording of the exercise with a special friend or lover or enjoy it alone. Keep in mind that all of us have flying dreams. When we are flying, so are many others. Why not invite them to fly with us?

> Position yourself comfortably and embrace that state of deep, inner peace. Let your personal space become clear, fresh and positive — all around you, and deep within you.
>
> Now begin to see in the distance, a star — far, far in the distance, as though you were looking through a magnificent telescope. You are seeing, experiencing, and feeling the wondrous light of a star, twinkling in the distance. It seems suspended against the blanket of that dark blue sky. Twinkling little rays of iridescent light are directed toward you. You become more and more captivated by the beauty of this special star — a star in your universe that is intensely focusing energy in your direction.
>
> Very shortly, you will become passionately enthralled, entranced by this special star. You sense that you have a very important relationship with this particular star.
>
> Slowly the star begins to move forward, moving closer to you and becoming larger and larger in your radius of vision. You feel the tingling, sparkling beams of light energy reaching and gently stroking your body. It is as though the star is embracing you as it moves closer and closer. How delightful it feels! Such a soft, gentle — but very intense — radiant light is shining directly upon you. This light is more beautiful than any you have ever

experienced before — pure, soft, gentle light with such intensity. The star moves closer and closer until a presence of light fills the whole room and shines all around you — relaxing, balancing, pleasuring.

Slowly now, another glorious delight begins. The energy rays from the star begin to merge with your own life energy. You feel the energy of the star within you. Your whole body is encircled and filled with light. Gently, the star begins to move up and away, slowly guiding you out of your body — ever so gently, entwined spirit and light, floating, drifting up and up. As the star drifts slowly, you move out of your body with the star — drifting up, up, up.

Surrounded by this gentle, wondrous light, you become completely free. You may, if you wish, look back and see your body lying comfortably, embraced and protected by the wondrous light. But you float free, floating up into the light, following the energy rays of the star. Twinkling now, you are feeling twinkling rays of starlight. It illuminates the night, guiding you, yet allowing you to go freely wherever you choose. Your movements are completely free. You can drift and float and in a twinkling of a starlit moment move from place to place. You can ascend far up above the trees, dive the depths of the ocean, fly around the world or sit on a mountain top. The choices are yours, and completely limitless. The entire universe is open to you.

But soon, you will meet your starmate. Bathed in radiant light, you now choose your personal journey of ecstasy. It feels so good. Radiant beams of starlight follow you wherever you go. You move, dancing toward your special starmate, loving and circling freely into a special rendezvous — twinkling, timeless movements in space — loving each and every movement. You are feeling more and more of the ecstasy that was always meant to be. The beauty of your starmate is beyond words and is magnified ten-thousand times by your own prisms of light energy. Reflections, swirling colors of pleasure, the music of wind chimes in starlight surround you.

Dancing sensuously with your starmate, and savoring the rapture, you begin a flight into ecstasy. Feel the increasing osmosis as billions of twinkling light rays explode together, like sparkling kisses — exploding orgasms of endless pleasure — merging souls drifting higher and higher. Higher and higher, until you experience a brilliant, beautiful climax of explosive starlight. Savor the pleasure, love the ecstasy — more and more — a glorious climax of peace and joy. You are pure, sensual energy — pleasure, goodness, love. You are the star. You are one with your starmate . . . twinkling, flowing spirits of universal love. All choices, all adventures, all freedoms, all pleasures and all knowledge is here NOW for you to embrace, embracing the ecstasy.

After you have fully experienced this wondrous starflight, you will find that the ecstasy remains as you drift back toward your body. Beams of light are following, drifting, cascading all around. You feel a wondrous glow as you begin to reunite with your body and you can feel yourself smiling, smiling. All the positive, wonderful benefits of this starflight remain with you for days, weeks — forever.

After you have completed your wonderful starflight, you may allow yourself to drift into a peaceful, natural sleep, sleeping comfortably for a while or you may choose to simply lie quietly for a few moments and then awaken. When you are ready to awaken, you will refocus your attention by counting slowly from one to ten, waking up more and more with each count. When you awaken you will continue to feel the lingering ecstasy of your heavenly starflight.

Affirmations

Spiritual bonding occurs when we invite intimacy and ecstasy into our lives. Affirmations will help you to relax with positive expectations and to accept the miracle of limitless intimacy. As you continue to create your own personal affirmations, it will become easy and automatic to think, speak and behave in positive ways. Complete the following sentences and notice that it is becoming easier and more natural to design your own positive affirmations.

1. Spiritual sex ....

2. I am ....

3. My starmate ....

4. Omnipresent joy ....

5. Spiritual bonding ....

6. .... limitless intimacy.

7. .... goodness and joy.

8. .... lingering ecstasy.

9. .... illusion of separateness.

10. .... osmosis of love.

Selected Readings

Bach, Richard. *The Bridge Across Forever*, Dell Publishing, New York, 1984.

Dossey, Larry. *Recovering The Soul: A Scientific and Spiritual Search,* Bantam Books, New York, 1989.

Evola, Julius. *The Metaphysics of Sex*, Inner Traditions International, New York, 1983.

Griscom, Chris. *Time Is An Illusion*, Simon and Schuster, New York, 1986.

Mitchell, Janet Lee. *Conscious Evolution*, Ballantine Books, New York, 1989.

Pearce, Joseph. *The Crack in the Cosmic Egg*, Julian Press, 1971.

Ring, Kenneth. *Heading Toward Omega*, William Morrow, Publishers, New York, 1984.

Reed, Henry. *Channeling Your Higher Self*, Warner Books, New York, 1989.

Reed, Henry. *Edgar Cayce On Mysteries of The Mind*, Warner Books, New York, 1989.

Stapledon, Olaf. *Star Maker*, J. L. Tarcher, Los Angeles, California, 1987.

Yatri. *Unknown Man*, Simon and Schuster, New York, 1988.

8

LIMITLESS INTIMACY

A Blissful State of Awareness

We can now open our minds, expand our consciousness and embrace the bliss of limitless intimacy. The yearning, loneliness and dissatisfaction of SAWNKI disappear as we begin to live in this state of expanded awareness. There is a delicious, lingering feeling — an ecstatic glow — that stays with us throughout our days. Limitless intimacy is like walking around in a state of rapture. Things around us seem to change in mysterious and wonderful ways. Life has more meaning, people are friendlier, tasks become easier and everything is more beautiful. Our perceptions are delightfully positive and sensitive; colors are brighter, music sweeter, food more delectable and our physical bodies prettier.

Limitless intimacy is a joyful state of spiritual awareness, an ongoing closeness, a way of relating with the true essence of life. In this state, we feel a sense of sexual aliveness and a spiritual oneness. And we begin to understand the true meaning of unconditional love. We enter this state by first uniting with our own spiritual centers and then bonding with the spiritual centers of other people.

The First Step

The first step towards limitless intimacy is uniting with our own souls. To become close to the spiritual self, we affirm that we are more than body, more than brain, more than behavior. We recognize that we are spiritual beings having a physical experience, not physical beings trying to have a spiritual experience. So regardless of outward appearances, we relate to an eternal center of love, goodness and infinite intelligence.

When we unite with our own spiritual centers, we develop an automatic awareness of self-worth. We feel a new type of self-confidence and self-love that is based on more than ego, more than achievement, more than physical appearance. And we recognize a tremendous inner power which is rooted in love and goodness. We can all live intimately with the spiritual self that we are. Living in communion with the spiritual self is often easier than we realize.

Simply by freeing the mind of external distractions, by becoming quiet and still, we can alter our consciousness and expand awareness into the spiritual realm. As we relax with positive expectations, our creative right brains are awakened and we return to the healthy child within. When we shift awareness to maximize pleasure, we are blessed with divine out-of-body experiences (OBEs). We can easily learn to create wonderful OBEs simply by practicing the fun exercises in this book.

Divine Mental Processes

OBEs demonstrate the existence of the mind separate from the brain and body. What is the mind? When we speak of mind, we refer to that indescribable essence which allows us to create our own destiny. Thomas Edison was once asked "What is electricity?" Edison was quiet for a long time and then replied, "My friend, electricity just is; don't question it, just use it!" So it is with the mind. It is a wonderful, powerful attribute of life that we can use to create limitless intimacy.

We all experience numerous changes or alterations in mental processes. Sleep, dreaming, visual imaging, concentrating and fantasying are common alterations of consciousness. The altered state of consciousness which we call OBE allows us to experience ourselves as pure spirit and strengthens our belief in personal immortality. With OBE, we can fly free from the restrictions of the body and know that we are indeed divine spirits. It is as though OBE introduces us to ourselves and shows us how to become intimate with our own souls. Then we are able to relate with other people in more loving and positive ways and can begin to move into the heavenly realm of limitless intimacy.

Sharing the Ecstasy

Limitless intimacy is living in a state of spiritual closeness with other people. Once we have united with our own spiritual centers, we can begin to share the ultimate intimacy with other people. Yes, there is a way to share the very essence of ourselves with another person. We call this shared altered state of consciousness, very simply, out-of-body sex or OBS.

Why do we call this special way of relating out-of-body sex, when it is a spiritual experience? As spiritual beings, we are filled with divine sexual energy and have limitless potential for ecstasy. OBS is an extremely pleasurable, sensuous encounter that has to be experienced to be understood. OBS may be accompanied by a physical orgasm of the body or may occur during physical sex. But OBS is more than physical sex — much more. Nevertheless, physical sex is a good comparison to OBS, because it helps us imagine an intense level of pleasure and intimacy. During OBS, the degree of ecstasy, level of communication and way of relating are so intense and wonderful that we cannot describe it with our limited language. The term OBS reminds us that we are referring to a spiritual experience which is also highly sexual by its very nature.

Perhaps it is time to stop creating these artificial separations. OBS shows us that spirituality and sexuality are inherently intertwined and inseparable. Just as OBE allows us to experience our own souls, OBS teaches us about our spiritual sexuality. Let's remember that there is a life force, a life-giving sexual energy, that flows freely between all of us. This divine energy is our pleasure source, creative life force and the magnet that draws us together.

Learning About Pleasure and Intimacy

OBS is a teacher who introduces us to the bliss of limitless intimacy. Relating during OBS may be as simple as the joyful awareness of another ethereal being. It may be an out-of-body touch or simply a wonderful form of communication. And sometimes OBS becomes an intense, overpowering union that evolves naturally into the ecstasy of spiritual bonding. But no matter what the form of OBS, it is always extremely pleasurable and very fulfilling, very satisfying.

OBS is about ecstasy, getting high and staying high, living life easily and very well. In fact, OBS is synonymous with feeling good; feeling very, very good. Part of feeling good and being happy is knowing that we can feel this way and that it is our natural right to be happy. Happiness is not something in limited supply that costs us dearly, unless we believe these negative myths. The very best thing we can ever do for ourselves and for everyone around us is to simply live in a state of divine happiness.

A big step towards affirming our right to pleasure and happiness is remembering how to really play again, becoming a small child — relaxed, free, spontaneous and natural. Think about a time when you were happy, young, alive and carefree. Was it so different from now? Were you happy because you didn't know better? Did someone tell you to stop having fun? Isn't it time to give yourself permission to play? Developing a right-brain awareness (feeling, laughing, singing, etc.) may be done by simply remembering how it is to be a young child. We are creators of life. And we can choose to create fun and happiness when we return to the healthy child within.

To say that OBS feels very nice is an understatement. OBS opens the door to limitless intimacy: pleasure without price, love without fear, ecstasy without prohibitions. And OBS is spiritual sex with total freedom — freedom from worries about disease, freedom from physical limitations, freedom from inhibitions. Those who practice OBS become more loving and more lovable, more alive and self-confident knowing that there is an abundance of love, pleasure, energy and ecstacy for all of us.

A Total Union of Souls

OBS is similar but unique for everyone, since we are all different. Each experience seems to provide whatever we need most at that moment. Note the tremendous flow of light and energy in the following OBS experience. This individual clearly felt the powerful flow of life-giving sexual energy, yet he also enjoyed great peace and tranquility. Prior to this OBS experience, the individual felt anxious, tired and unfocused. Afterwards, he felt relaxed, peaceful and centered with strong positive feelings that lingered for more than a week.

> *It was so nice. There were giant doors that opened up in this big hall, and I was surrounded by light and the flutter of a lot of wings, like real slow waves of light. I got the distinct impression of angels. And then I sort of became a star, and saw energy shooting out of my star. I was emitting energy and there was energy from somewhere else that was coming into me as light. It was almost like drops of light, like images*

of rain. I was moving energy, moving white light. I had form something like a human body but made of starlight.

My lover was another ethereal being like myself. Our bodies and light could merge in every way; sometimes it was two-dimensional, like flat planes, then it would become three-dimensional and move around. The qualities of whatever made up the light were in phase, coherent like laser light. Every particle knew every other particle and they were all perfectly compatible. Each particle had a consciousness of itself. All the particles of one being knew and merged with the particles of the other being. There was a comfort without desire. It was not lustful in the usual sense. There was a physical interaction but not an urgency. It was much more fulfilling somehow.

I had other images of simple ocean animals intertwined in a perfect unity. They were completely malleable and flexible, intertwined so that you could not tell there were two animals. And then there was an image of the blending of two strands of bread becoming one loaf in the baking process. At some point in the process there is a total union of the two strands of same material, which is like the union of the two starlike beings.

I was really struck at how extremely relaxed I was. I felt comfortable and warm. It was very peaceful. There was a lot of light, incredible light. It was real pervasive and warm, very penetrating. When our two ethereal beings merged, they could separate at any time, but I'm not real sure if what went in is what came out. There was a merging with a transfer of energy. It was intensely penetrating, but there was gentleness in the exchange. There was an ecstatic merging with a wonderful peacefulness, very very fulfilling.

This individual's beautiful OBS experience helps us understand limitless intimacy. Note that "each particle has a consciousness of itself," just as we humans all have a consciousness of ourselves. In addition, "every particle knew every other particle and they were all compatible." So it will become with limitless intimacy! We will each know the essence of every other being and we will all be compatible. We are all like twisted strands of warm, rising bread. At some point in the growth process, we will experience a total union. And then we will begin to understand that we are like interconnected cells. We are not separate; we are not alone. We are ONE — energy, love, ecstasy, goodness — ONE. OBS, especially the more advanced level of spiritual bonding, shows us this type of total union and teaches us how to live in a state of limitless intimacy.

Spiritual Bonding

Spiritual bonding is a kind of spiritual explosion that puts us into the state of limitless intimacy. It is a total, complete merging of souls that has been described as the ultimate orgasm. The ecstasy we share goes far beyond what we are capable of sharing on a purely physical level. When we bond in this way, there is a tremendous fusion of light and pleasure and goodness. The osmosis of energy we share during spiritual bonding creates unity, a oneness which allows us to recognize that we are love. And the communication is so perfect that it goes beyond words, beyond mental telepathy. It's as though there is nothing left to say because it is all understood.

Spiritual bonding and OBS are real experiences and much more than abstract concepts written on a piece of paper. They can be learned by doing the exercises in this book. But they are not learned by reading and thinking, just as a musical instrument is not learned by studying music theory. We learn to play an instrument by practicing, by doing. This is how we develop most of our skills. OBS and spiritual bonding are skills that we can easily develop with practice. Actually, ordinary physical sex is more difficult to learn than out-of-body sex. And spiritual bonding occurs naturally when we learn to share OBS.

Steps Along the Way

To develop our skills for living in a state of limitless intimacy, we begin with ourselves. OBE helps us become close to our inner self, to unite with the spiritual part of ourselves. Then OBS helps us become close to others, to unite spiritually with others. Spiritual bonding, an advanced type of OBS, allows us to merge completely with the soul of another person; it puts us in the state of limitless intimacy. As we practice loving ourselves and others in these wonderful ways, we can begin to live in a state of limitless intimacy. And the best news is that anytime we feel ourselves losing touch with limitless intimacy, we can return to OBE and OBS. The doors of our consciousness will then open and we will again become centered in love.

These miracles happen when we realize that we can have it all: ecstasy, happiness and inner peace; simultaneous intimacy and individuality; wholly integrated spiritual and physical worlds. Yes, heaven on earth, the cherished garden of Eden is ours. We can experience life calmly centered, yet feel thrillingly alive and excited. And best of all, there is no price to pay. It has already been paid for. We have already done OBS, all of us. We have been there. We will be there again. We can be there now. Actually we are now evolving rapidly into that higher state of consciousness which allows us to live in a state of limitless intimacy.

Living in Heaven

There is a painting by Hieronymus Bosch called "Ascending into the Empyrean." Empyrean refers to the highest reaches of heaven. It is an inspiring painting. And yet heaven is not a place "out there." Heaven comes from within and dwells within. It is an inseparable part of all of us. It is our home. It is where we all come from. And OBS reintroduces us to heaven in a dramatic and delightful way.

The facets of heaven are easily accessible through a variety of conscious and unconscious expressions. The movie "Made in Heaven" evoked a wonderful mood conducive to OBS for us. And we often enjoy other powerful forms of communication — dance, music, painting, poetry, to name a few. These are all expressions of an emotion, an idea, an experience. Art forms are so beautiful. But what if we could feel what the dancer feels, the painter or the singer at their very moment of inspiration and creation? Sometimes art succeeds in doing just this. Now go one small step farther and imagine what it would be like to feel the artist's very soul without needing the medium, or see through the painter's eyes, or hear with the poet's ears. This is the magical realm of OBS.

Perhaps one of the most important points of this book is that there exists a level of communication way beyond what we would normally have in an ordinary relationship. With OBS, there is a direct, perfect and instantaneous sharing of our feelings and thoughts, our very essence. This level of sharing creates spiritual unity, a state of peaceful compatibility that shows us that we can be totally intimate without giving up anything. OBS is a translation of love into action and experience. It is real. We can touch it and be touched by it. OBS is a state of being that embraces the big picture. It is a way of hearing beyond the noise, of seeing through the haze, of sensing the next evolutionary leap. Limitless intimacy is that next jump to a higher consciousness that we have all been anticipating.

In this altered state of consciousness that we call OBS, so many apparent opposites are reconciled: freedom and intimacy, separateness and oneness, sex and spirit. OBS is so good for us. Its harmonizing influence lingers for days after each experience. How many relationships degenerate in the perceived battle between freedom and intimacy? OBS transforms this illusory conflict into a positive affirmation of both unity and individuality. It is a way of seeing the whole and all its facets simultaneously, a way of recognizing that separation is artificial, an illusion. We are like facets of a diamond, beautiful, sparkling energy cells.

When we are spiritually illuminated, we reflect love and goodness. But we do not reflect alone. Like facets of a diamond, we reflect most beautifully when we are bonded together.

Connecting and Loving

There is a very strong connection between all of us, an undeniable sense of the presence of other souls. Have you ever thought you were alone, then felt someone else nearby? You had no physical clues, just a feeling, but you were right? We can expand this kind of perception or connection into OBS. When we practice OBS, our perceptions become more acute and we may begin to see auras, anticipate feelings, predict events or look farther into the eyes of others.

As we begin to live in a state of limitless intimacy, we can look at others and see their true essence — the spiritual self that resides within. So regardless of physical or behavioral illusions, regardless of outward appearances, we behold beauty and goodness in everyone. With this increased awareness, we have new understandings, our differences become enjoyable and we have an automatic ability to empathize. Our foolish conflicts fade into the nothingness from which they came and we enjoy peace and harmony. Enthusiasm and ecstasy flow freely between us. And we can honestly say to each other "I behold the spiritual goodness that is you; I embrace it and unite with it."

Have you ever questioned love or felt unloved? You are not alone. Each of us has questioned the meaning of love and sought the fulfillment of love. We all want to feel love, to know that we're loved, and to share an intimate ecstasy. This is our dream. OBS, especially spiritual bonding, propels our dream into reality. It gives us a new type of love, a complete fulfillment with intense ecstasy and a deeper level of intimacy. Once we have shared OBS, the word love takes on new meanings. When we merge as spiritual beings, we become love and goodness. The presence of love begins to fill our daily lives and we are extended into a universal love — a unified, omnipresent love. Living with this kind of love is living in limitless intimacy.

The Unborn Potential

With limitless intimacy, we feel omnipresent love and an increasing sense of brotherhood. Life becomes more meaningful and easier. Rather than struggling laboriously through our day, we have a feeling of ease. We feel lighter and can almost float through the day, but we float with purpose, meaning and direction rather than drifting aimlessly. There is a carefreeness that comes from spiritual understanding and a unity with others that evolves from spiritual bonding.

Within each of us is the unborn potential of limitless intimacy, and we all have the priviledge of giving birth to it. Limitless intimacy is conceived during a sexual encounter of souls. Spiritual bonding is a complete merging of souls, an orgasmic osmosis of sexual energy. It is a climax of pleasure that is so intense, yet paradoxically very calming and nurturing. Spiritual bonding is like being a contented, happy infant in the womb, while simultaneously being a joyous, expectant mother who is giving life to her baby.

After we have learned to enjoy OBE, we can easily bond with a friend or lover and share the ecstasy of OBS. Then we can expand the OBS community to create abundant pleasure for everyone. We can extend the intimacy and sexual ecstasy to all, including those individuals we label sick, old, disabled, ugly, and so forth. Let's remember that we are all beautiful and healthy in our divine spiritual forms. With OBS, every soul can be embraced in a vibrant blending of sex and spirit. OBS also allows us to embrace those who have already died and those who are not yet born. As we enlarge the circle of those with whom we are spiritually bonded, we can move into our heaven on earth.

An Empathic Group Experience

The following statements are from a group experience of five individuals who shared an altered state of consciousness and then linked empathically. Their experiences were very rich and complex. Here are a few of their comments, not necessarily in the order they were spoken.

There are so many things to remember. There's something I want to remember but I can't. It seems like there was so much, and there are things that are lost for me. It feels like I left for a long time.

There was a longing, beckoning calling of a blend of you two women in a diaphanous gown on a hilltop at night. The figure had features of both of you. There was moonlight. I felt this pull quite strongly at different times.

You had a lot of physiological stuff going on, did you know that? For one thing, your hands were trembling a lot, and then your whole body. I could see you trembling even though my eyes were closed.

I guess you stopped talking for a period of time and I said, "Where am I?" Then my right side started vibrating. It was almost like I was asleep and dreaming and waking up from a dream all at the same time. It seemed like hours went by.

When we first started, I closed my eyes and could still see you. And it wasn't just a negative image, but multiple images of different layers of tissue and different temperatures, different colors. It was fun to play with. At times it was so bright that it hurt my eyes.

There were wind chimes and shafts of light, like underwater. Intense metallic green and blue colors, bright and shiny, were like Christmas wrappers. I felt like I was in a cartoon because you can do anything in a cartoon. It was fun and very free feeling.

A crystal ball moved toward us and took us inside and thousands of multicolored streamers flew out like from a cruise ship leaving port. The ball was like a Faberge egg, but bigger and more complex with a lot of translucent, shifting oval shapes clustered around it, and lit from within. It was beautiful and liquid, and we were all in it.

I saw streamers of bright colors. We were discrete colors, changing. You, your voice was a star and there were projections from the star. The star seemed like a bubble. As it moved towards us, it took us inside of it, and that was when streamers began to fall and there were just thousands of them. It was very beautiful.

An Aurora Borealis fragmented into millions of dancing lines of light. Wind chimes and starlight went into your eyes and into your body. Love feelings surrounded everybody in the room. Everything was soft and then vibrating. It felt real tingly. I could feel the warmth of halos of golden light. I heard waves, surf. We were golden beings on a bluish purple background.

There is an energy force that runs through everyone. We were an energy form, a field that can manifest in any shape. Your face was there, my face was there — a lot of changing around and commingling. All of us were connected by lines of light. I remember I was connected to your upper lip by a shaft of laser light; it was really nice. We were all connected by changing lines of light. It was almost a technological image.

During the experience I had a real feeling of closeness or proximity to everybody. When I returned to the room, to my body, we were real spread out. It was surprising.

> There was a whole lot going on; it's almost overwhelming to try to recount. I had to come back to my body from time to time to catalog and store the images so I could tell you about them later. And yet a lot is lost. I mean, I still can feel that more happened, but I just can't describe it. It happens so quickly, too fast for any recorder I know of.

One very interesting aspect of this group experience is the commonality that went beyond the suggestions of the leader. Also, a number of the images and sounds were felt before the leader ever suggested them. It was almost as if the experience came first, as if it were writing the script. According to the members of the group, the experience became independent of the leader almost immediately after it began.

Expanding Into Limitless Intimacy

OBS promotes growth on every level and helps us become beautiful — physically, emotionally, behaviorally and socially beautiful. As we practice OBS, we begin to view worry and fear as ridiculous. We develop a kind of gracious acceptance of our humanness, our so-called flaws, mistakes and limitations. And there is an acceptance of others. Our overemphasis on looks, physical imperfections, aging and so forth seems silly as we begin to embrace each other spiritually. With OBS, we see the little human games we play and understand that they have very little validity when we rise to the level of limitless intimacy.

OBS expands our perceptions and allows us to see more clearly. Do we create our world through our perceptions and beliefs? Isn't it time to change our focus? Perhaps it is less a task of changing wrongs in a world which seems lost and more a task of seeing things correctly. Our distorted perceptions and false beliefs have often limited us and caused unhappiness. Nearsighted concepts such as jealousy, envy, scarcity, ugliness and badness simply vanish when we embrace the wider vision given by OBS. As we move into limitless intimacy, myths of lack and limitation will disappear and we will finally be able to create abundance and prosperity for all.

In the afterglow of OBS, we see more beauty within and around us and enjoy people more. Other people also enjoy us more because we are happy, relaxed, accepting and curious about our world and everything in it. Living longer, better, fuller, and richer lives — sound too good to be true? When we are all spiritually bonded, we will live in ecstasy. War, loneliness and poverty will disappear; unconditional love and universal peace will be a reality. As we embrace each other, the bliss of limitless intimacy embraces us.

Pathways to Limitless Intimacy

The exercises in this book are practical and also fun. You have the freedom to choose the ones you like best and to adapt them in whatever ways feel good to you. However it is important to do the exercises. Each exercise is a pathway which leads you closer to the bliss of limitless intimacy. Before beginning the following beautiful journey, you may want to relax with a simple relaxation exercise.

> Feel the light centered within you, the light that is you, the light that you are. Feel the love and warmth of this light and allow it to radiate peace and happiness. It feels so good, so wonderful, caressing every cell in your body and mind. Everything feels perfect and right, natural and flowing free. Allow the light to flood your awareness with joyful energy, and to carry your consciousness like an iridescent droplet in curtains of warm tropical rain. See the rain in the full daylight of a bright and friendly sun, twisting transparent sheets of shimmering rain. Hear the happy sound of the rain. Feel the tingling massage as thousands of penetrating raindrops invigorate your skin ever so gently. Allow the sunlight reflected in each drop to enter your body, nourishing and warming it.

Feel the glow of this light within your forehead, within your heart, your solar plexus and deep inside your sexual organs. Allow the light to spread gently throughout your entire body. You begin to glow from the inside out and you are becoming surrounded by a sphere of loving radiance. Now allow your light, your awareness, to expand into the universe. As you expand, you draw more and more energy from the limitless source of all light. Your freedom and joy and power are boundless as you become one with this source.

As you expand to become a radiant star in the heavens, you realize that the light from all suns streams from this single source. And you are inseparable from that life-giving stream of light — a light containing all colors, all sounds, all patterns past and future. Your awareness is linked to all sentience in this light. You and your brothers and sisters, lovers and friends are all linked to this same ocean of light. Through this channel, communication and understanding are perfect and immediate.

Feel now, the presence of your lover — that special vibration which is so unique and wonderful. Allow your awareness to focus on this perfect love. Allow the illusion of separation to slip easily away like satin sheets falling from a bed. See the smile in your lover's eyes as you both meet in a swirling dance of ecstasy. Allow your awareness to merge with your lover's awareness and begin to share your deepest, truest feelings. Touch your lover and feel the ecstasy of being touched. Stroking gently, exploring each others' uniqueness — the intricacies, elegance and beauty. Trusting, opening, sharing freely, appreciating the perfection manifest within each of you.

Feel the strong, insistent contact of your sexual energy. The ecstasy flows back and forth between you, surging through the raceway of your being like powerful ocean currents. Let your physical sexuality freely express the fullness of your spiritual and emotional love. Allow your bodies to merge. Allow your spirits to merge. Allow your merging minds to dance and drift. This is the most wonderful thing that has ever happened to you. You are trusting, accepting and allowing yourself to become lost in it.

Feel the power and passion of the universe thundering within your shared being, like unending waves of crashing, iridescent surf. Allow this sensation to flood your consciousness, giving life and energy beyond measure. See this vibrant energy illuminate your lover in exquisitely jeweled colors and patterns, as your lover perceives the prismatic light within you. The origin of this light suffuses through and around each of you as you merge into a twin being, a divinely spiritual radiance of perfect knowing. You are One — a creature of light creating a uniquely beautiful song to resonate with the primal forces of the universe.

Thrill to an intimacy beyond mortal possibility, a simultaneous perception of all that you and your lover are individually and together. Experience each harmonious facet and the whole, integrated as one living entity. Step outside of time and perceive past and future connected in a circular continuum. Accept the gifts that are yours, the gifts that have been patiently waiting for you — the gift of complete and perfect intimacy, the gift of peace, and the gift of love.

Allow all aspects of your beings to merge in a harmonious flow of sexual energy. Allow your physical bodies to mirror this spiritual ecstasy. Feel it vibrate inside of you like a thousand stringed instruments. Let it pulse through every fiber in your body and mind. Let the feelings overwhelm you in a flash-flood of brilliant light and sound, until you are the light and you are the sound. Know that you can be here whenever you need to. Now just continue to flow into the rapture, drifting and dissolving into infinite bliss.

Allow yourself plenty of time to savor this experience before refocusing your attention. When you are ready to refocus, count out loud, slowly counting from one to ten and waking up more and more with each count. The ecstasy will remain with you after awakening. You can enjoy all of the exercises in this book again and again. Each exercise will bless you and lead you further into the ecstasy of limitless intimacy.

Affirmations

At some point, limitless intimacy becomes an "I am" experience. Soon we will each feel free to affirm: "I am the essence of love." "I am the source of love." "I am love." And we will also affirm goodness, pleasure, beauty and peace. Affirmations of "I am" will be accompanied by affirmations of "You are" and affirmations of "We are". With these affirmations, we recognize our ONENESS and celebrate the ecstasy of limitless intimacy.

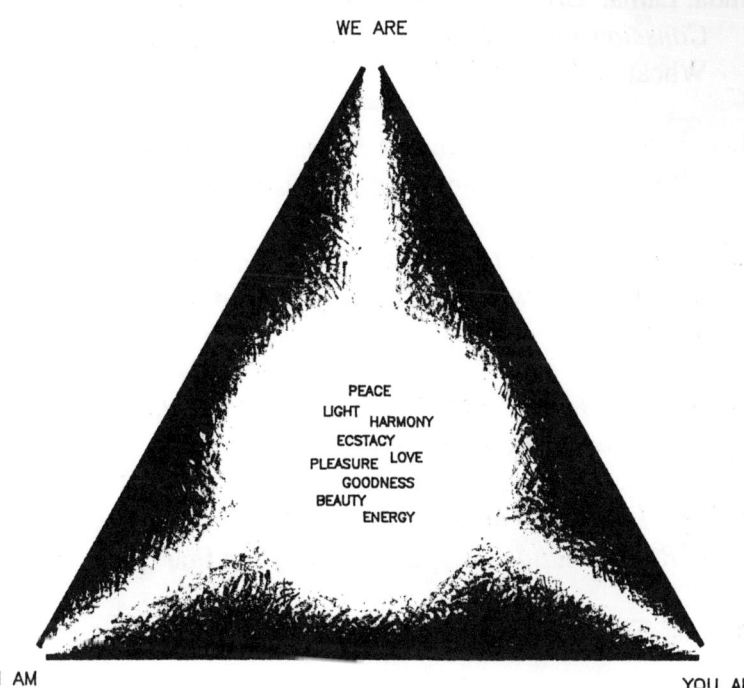

Selected Readings

Bach, Richard. *The Bridge Across Forever*, Dell Publishing, New York, 1984.

Bach, Richard. *One*, William Morrow, New York, 1988.

Curtis, Donald. *Daily Power for Joyful Living*, Wilshire Books, No. Hollywood, California, 1974.

Dossey, Larry. *Recovering the Soul: A Scientific and Spiritual Search*, Bantam Books, New York, 1989.

Govinda, Lama. *Creative Meditation and Multi-dimensional Consciousness*, Theosophical Publishing House, Wheaton, Illinois, 1976.

Mesher, Alan. *Journey of Love: A Formula for Mastery of Miracles*, Quartus Foundation, Austin, Texas, 1982.

Shakti-Gawain. *Return to the Garden: A Journey of Discovery*, New World Library, San Rafael, California, 1989.

Starke, Walter. *Homesick for Heaven: You Don't Have to Wait*, Guadalupe Press, Boerne, Texas, 1988.

Stern, Jess. *Intimates Through Time: Edgar Cayce's Mysteries of Reincarnation*, Harper and Row, San Francisco, 1989.

Stern, Jess. *Soul Mates*, Bantam Books, New York, 1984.

APPENDIX A

Ineffability

When something you experience simply cannot be adequately communicated with the normal media (words, pictures, mathematics, etc.), then we say the experience is ineffable. We have collected a small group of quotations that address the concept of ineffability and spiritual experience. Even the simplest feeling can be inexpressible. The problem of ineffability may arise from the structure of the brain. Our language is essentially a left-brain, abstract, linear process, and it has trouble translating right-brain processes into something meaningful. The solution requires a better integration of left and right brain functions, and ultimately an ability to run both at the same time.

"...what can be handed on to others is not the vision itself, but the inadequate symbols in which the seer tries to represent what he has seen and to preserve it in his memory." 1

"If any one, seeing God, knows what he sees, it is by no means God that he sees, but something created and knowable." Lao Tse. 2

"It cannot be expressed by means of anything else, just because it is so primary and elementary a datum in our psychical life, and therefore only definable through itself." 3

"...a light of which I cannot speak except to those who would know already of what might then be said — beyond our words, where speech itself is superfluous, a knowing beyond the clouds of all unknowing, an answer beyond all questioning." 4

"All I have written is like straw." 5

1. Inge, W. R. *Mysticism in Religion*, Hutchinson & Co., London, 1947.

2. Cheney, Seldon. *Men Who have Walked with God*, Knoph, New York, 1945.

3. Otto, Rudolf. *The Idea of the Holy*, Oxford University Press, Oxford, England, 1923.

4. Pearce, Joseph. *the crack in the cosmic egg*, Julian Press, New York, 1971.

5. St. Thomas Aquinas, an eleventh century philosopher priest, after a vision he had late in life. This is the last thing he ever wrote.

APPENDIX B

How to Tape Record An Exercise

Professionally recorded tapes are available from the publisher. To order tapes, refer to the order form in the back of this book.

If you wish to make your own recordings of the written exercises in this book, just follow our simple instructions. Such tapes are for your personal use only and you are prohibited by copyright from selling or distributing any material from this book. If you wish to record your own tapes, you will need a recorder with a remote microphone and several sixty or ninety minute tapes (thirty to forty-five minutes per side).

Choose a leisure time when you are feeling relaxed and peaceful. Choose a location that is protected from noise. Turn the telephone off and make sure you will be free from interruptions. You may play soft, instrumental music in the background if desired.

Place the microphone close to your mouth, but keep it distant enough to avoid harsh breathing sounds. Speak softly, slowly and calmly. Pause at the end of sentences and phrases to allow your breathing to remain natural and easy. Also, remember that pauses help promote relaxation for the listener. So, let it be a slow, leisurely process.

Experiment with your equipment, so that you can determine the proper sound level for your recording. If the level is too high your tape may be distorted, or if the level is too low the background hiss may be objectionable. While recording, avoid touching the microphone, cable, stand or recorder. If you are wearing a lapel microphone, sit still. The quality of your tape may be improved if you use a directional microphone with a soft foam windscreen.

Take your time, relax and enjoy the process. The first recording is often very good, so don't rewind the tape and record over the previous recording, unless it was absolutely ruined by equipment or operator failure. It may be better to rewind to the beginning of a mistake and record over that part only. You may reduce start-up noises by using the pause button.

Each exercise has been carefully designed to be positive and enjoyable. So read each exercise as it written and avoid extemporaneous comments. In general, it is best to avoid improvising or changing the text, unless a word or phrase really bothers you. You may, however, speak with the first person pronoun or the second person pronoun ("I am now becoming relaxed." or "You are now becoming relaxed."). We have found that most people prefer to use the second person pronoun.

Start with the beginning exercises and progress slowly to the more advanced ones. If you dislike a particular exercise, skip it and choose another one. Just relax and have fun with the exercises.

Always record a refocusing or alertness exercise at the end of each tape. This alertness exercise is sometimes called a wake-up exercise, but the term wake-up is a misnomer, since we are only relaxed and ordinarily not asleep. Still, it is important to refocus our attention and be alert before resuming normal household chores and so on. The following alertness exercise should always be recorded on each tape following the regular exercise.

It is now time to focus your attention on becoming alert and fully awake. You will become more and more alert, as I count from one to ten, so that by the time I reach the count of ten, you will be wide awake and very alert. You will feel refreshed and very happy. Counting now . . . one . . . two . . . becoming more alert with each count . .

It is now time to focus your attention on becoming alert and fully awake. You will become more and more alert, as I count from one to ten, so that by the time I reach the count of ten, you will be wide awake and very alert. You will feel refreshed and very happy. Counting now . . . one . . . two . . . becoming more alert with each count . . . three . . . four . . . feeling more and more energy . . . five . . . six . . . more and more alert . . . seven . . . eight . . . it feels so good to be waking up . . . nine . . . ten, wide awake and alert.

ORDER FORM

Name_____

Street_____

City/State/Zip_____

Please send me _____ copies of *Limitless Intimacy*. I have enclosed $15 per book, which includes all shipping, handling and applicable taxes.

Please send me _____ sets of cassette tapes (each set includes most of the exercises in the book) at $45 each, which includes all shipping, handling, and applicable taxes.

Total amount enclosed is: $ _____

Make checks or money orders payable to:

**Elysian Press
Dept A1
Box 180158
Dallas, Texas 75218**

Telephone orders accepted at **214- 321- 6996**.

Color prints of the original cover art are available.

Book distributors call for bulk prices.

Allow four weeks for delivery.

Dr. Narecia Hamrick is a psychologist in private practice, who is highly skilled in the integration of analytical, behavioral and intuitive approaches to psychotherapy. She is well known for her breadth and depth of experience as a hypnotherapist and as a trainer and supervisor of interns in psychotherapy and hypnotherapy. Dr. Hamrick has lectured extensively, chaired large symposia, taught at major universities, and served as Coordinator of Intern Training. An honors graduate from Southern Methodist University, she received her Ph.D. from North Texas University magna cum laude.

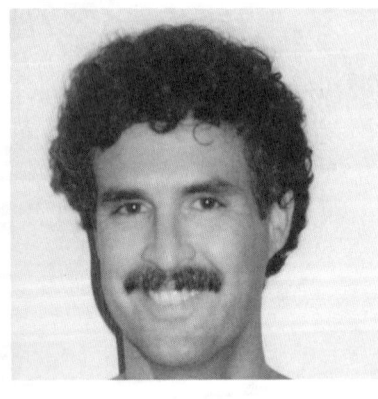

Grant Bingeman is a rare Renaissance man who has a gift for combining science and art in creative endeavors. He has been honored as a guest lecturer both nationally and internationally. In addition he has served as a contributing editor for a trade journal and published more than 50 articles. Mr. Bingeman is an electrical engineer who graduated from the University of Virginia. As a volunteer counselor for a crisis center in Texas, Mr. Bingeman utilized his talents of intuitive understanding and empathy in the analysis of human problems.